MY LIFE REVISITED

*An updated version of the book 'My Life'
by Bobby Ball first published in 1993*

This book is dedicated to
My Grandchildren

MY LIFE REVISITED

BOBBY BALL

Foreword by Tommy Cannon

Harvest Fields

Published by Harvest Fields,
Unit 17, Churchill Business Park, Churchill Road,
Doncaster BN1 2TF

ISBN 978-1-903905-30-2

A RoperPenberthy Publishing Ltd production
for Harvest Fields

Cover design by Angie Moyler

Typeset by Avocet Typeset, Chilton, Aylesbury, Bucks
Printed in the United Kingdom by Cox & Wyman Ltd,
Reading, Berkshire

CONTENTS

FOREWORD

Fancy me, Tommy Cannon, writing a foreword about a book. Well, what can I say? Nothing! Because I have never written one before.

No, seriously, I know this will give me great pleasure to write, because it is about my partner and friend Bobby Ball.

Where do I start? Well, I suppose the best place to start is at the beginning. I first met Bobby at Boden Trailers engineering factory in Oldham. I was the new boy standing by the clocking-in machine, when in came this little character and said, 'Hello cock.' He was the first and only person to speak to me out of five hundred men. By the way, I make no excuse for the terminology of the word 'cock' because in Oldham it means pal or friend. And this friendship has lasted for thirty years.

To talk about Bobby before he became a Christian isn't easy. The moods he had at times were unbearable. He found it difficult to talk to me about what was troubling him, so I in turn wouldn't talk to him. After several days one of us would say something daft to break the tension. I know a lot of it was to do with us becoming 'stars' (for the want of a better word) and the immense pressure we were under. Also material things had become more important than real life itself. Well, that's enough of the past. He has now come out of his dark tunnel and into a bright light.

In 1986 Bobby became a born-again Christian. To write about the change in him would take me forever, but I thought he was a crackpot when he first told me and obviously I found it hard to believe, but the results of Bobby finding his faith has led to us becoming true friends and we are now closer than brothers. He is easier to work with and if I have any problems he not only listens but he also tries to help. That is some change I can tell you, and it's good to know that a man I have known and worked with for over forty years will be with me or me with him when we take our last breath on this earth.

Now a little bit about myself. I also have made a commitment to God and have become a born-again Christian. It is the biggest change in my life, and I have to tell you it's FANTASTIC!

I am very proud to have put forward these few words for this book. It will not be remarkable for its literary style or a deep understanding about the mysteries of life but for a simple truthfulness of a man who made a commitment that changed his life. Anyone reading this book, Christian or not, will find it fascinating, and maybe, just maybe, us think for a moment about God.

ACKNOWLEDGEMENTS

Here are some people I would like to acknowledge without whose help this book would not have been published

James Catford   for allowing me the opportunity to write
Tommy Cannon   for his support and faith in me
Keith Chadwick   for just being a friend
My Children   for giving me years of happiness
My Grandchildren   for keeping that happiness going

But most of all I would like to thank my wife Yvonne, for her patience and love through all the years, but more than that I want to thank her for being my wife

Bobby Ball

Chapter 1

'Our Bobby'

Life for me began many, many years ago, so many in fact that I am sure that Dinosaurs roamed the earth when I entered this mortal coil. I was born on January 28th 1944 in the Boundary Park Hospital, Oldham. I was born the youngest of three children to Bob and May Harper. My father must have been overjoyed when I was born because apparently he had told my mother that she must keep having children until he had a boy. His first two children were girls so when I came along it must have been the happiest day of his life. At last he had a son, a child that would fulfill his own dreams of being a great sportsman. Oh, how his dreams would be shattered.

On my fathers birth certificate he was christened Bob, so when I was born they decided to go posh and christen me Robert. My father must have thought that Bob wasn't a good enough name for his only son. So it's funny now because it is only my family who call me Robert, everyone else calls me Bob. My father was a small man, with a big heart, standing no more than five feet tall, but as he used to say 'you never get a soft Jack Russell.' This is true because looking back he was like a Jack Russell terrier. He was small and wiry and very strong with a sense of quickness about him. He always wore his favorite possessions, his flat cap and his clogs and the only time he took off his flat cap is when he went to bed. The picture in my memory of my dad is of this little man walking down the street in his flat cap and clogs, whistling loudly as if he didn't have care in the world, which he obviously did. It's strange but I never really appreciated my dad until he had passed away. I loved my dad and one of the biggest regrets of my life is that I didn't tell him I loved him enough. Oh, if only we could go back.

My mother, what can I say about my mother? I think it was from her that I got my sense of humor and love of music, although some people may argue that I haven't got one. She was a small woman only standing 4 feet 11 inches and she always seemed to be smiling. I can see her now in my mind standing there in her flowered apron (my mother called it a pinny) with her jet black hair and she always seemed to have a laughing twinkle in her eye as if she knew something the world didn't. Life for my sisters and me as children could be very hard. We lived on the poverty line and I am still amazed at my mother's inner strength, at how she managed to feed and keep us clothed. To this day I am still astonished that she managed it. Home for us was a small, recently condemned house; high in the hills overlooking a little village in Lancashire named Shaw. Shaw was a village that was well known in Lancashire for weaving cotton. My father used to tell me that there were more cotton mills in Shaw than anywhere else in Lancashire. Due the modernization they have all gone now, but when I was a boy the looming, dark satanic mills with their huge chimneys climbing high into the sky gave Shaw a personality of its own. From where we lived high in the hills we could look down over Shaw and to me it was a wondrous place. For a child it was a place of adventure and love and simplicity. I think that it's sometimes sad how time has to move on. I believe that here in the 21st century we have lost something from the past. Life is too fast now to be able to enjoy the simple things; or maybe that is just age that is talking.

As with most houses of that era, the one that we lived in also had a character of its own. It was a strange house with only one external door which led directly into the kitchen. The kitchen had a flagged floor which ran all the way through the downstairs of the house. Underneath a small window stood a shallow stone sink which was about two inches deep and this was called a slop stone. I remember this sink very well because it's were my mother used to stand singing to herself as she washed up the dishes and did all the weekly clothes washing. No such things as washing machines then for poor families. In the corner of the kitchen were the stairs that led up to the one and only bedroom we had, and in the other corner of the kitchen stood a white-washed door that led down to my nightmare, the cellar. The kitchen led into a small living room that had about eight little windows that overlooked the fields surrounding us. We didn't have curtains because the walls had deteriorated so much that it was impossible to attach anything to them. I remember my father once trying to put some curtains up and the bricks and plaster started to fall down, so he never bothered trying again. He just said 'It is better to have bricks and mortar than curtains'. We had an old un-varnished table in the centre of the room with news-paper on it for a table-cloth. And I remember my mother changing the newspaper every time we sat down to eat. She used to laugh and say 'Well, at least we will have something to read while we are eating, I'll bet posh folks don't have that luxury.' But underneath her laughter I suspect she secretly longed for her own brand-new table-cloth with roses sewn around the edges. Against the far wall stood a magnificent old cast-iron fireplace, with ovens at both sides and a stand where a kettle would sit all day keeping warm for the ever-ready cup of tea. Today that fire-place would be worth a fortune to an antique dealer, but in the early fifties everyone wanted the new tiled fire-places that had become fashionable, so the old cast-iron fire-places were thrown away like some old decrepit thing of the past. What a shame that sometimes what we think of as new and modern is sometimes not as good as the old. I loved that old fireplace. Late at night, in the eerie glow of gas light, my sisters Mavis and Sylvia would sit in the ovens and I would sit on my mother's knee in front of a roaring fire while she told us endless stories of when she was a child, and then we would hear my fathers clogs and his whistle as he came home from a night at the local pub.

Upstairs there was one bedroom and a small landing at the top of the stairs that would just fit a double bed, and that is where my sisters slept, and I, being the only boy, slept in the bedroom with my mother and father. My bed and my domain was a small single bed pushed into the far corner of the room. At night, whenever it started to rain my mother had a ritual. She would get as many pots and pans as she could and place them strategically around the room. I used to watch fascinated as she looked up and the ceiling and then continue to place her pots and pans in exact positions on the floor. Then when it started to rain, the raindrops would start to come in and the different- sized raindrops would hit the different sized pots and pans, creating a kind of nature's symphony. My mother seemed to know which raindrops would hit which pot or pan. How did she know that? Many a time I would lie awake in the dead of night listening to the raindrops music, with the occasional snore for my dad to give the music some bass.But the centre of my imagination was the cellar. It was a dark dank place with no lighting and there were about twelve stone steps that led down into the dark abyss. In my imagination and to me that was real, there were at least about twenty different monsters hiding in different corners, waiting just to get me. I imagined them whispering to one another, 'Here comes Bobby, get him, get him.' I'm sure I met a few of them disguised as humans, as I got older. The cellar was defiantly a hell-hole for me when I was a child and I tried my hardest to avoid it like the plague.

It was my eldest sister, Sylvia's job to light the fire before my mother and father got home from work. And where do you think the coal was kept to light the fire? That's right, you've guessed, the cellar. And who do you think always had to get the coal? You've guessed right again. Me! No matter how much I argued or begged and pleaded, I always ended up having to go down into the monster's lair and get the coal. Eventually I got the task of getting past the monsters down to a fine art. My biggest ally in getting the coal was my other sister, Mavis, a red –haired girl, who I am sure, could have fought any boy in Shaw and won. She was fearless, which was great for me because she fought most of my battles when I was a child. She sort of looked after her little brother if you know what I mean. She was, and still is, one of my closest friends. She was always there when I needed her and for that I will be eternally grateful. Anyway, I digress. Back to the saga of getting the coal. My sister, Sylvia would say, in her 'I'm the oldest voice', 'Robert, go and get the coal.' I would have a tantrum, then I would promise to run errands for her, and finally I would look at her with eyes that would melt an iceberg, but it was all to no avail. I knew that I would have to get the coal. I would then look at our Mavis, who knew exactly what was going to ask, before I would even have asked her.

'Mavis,' I would ask, 'will you stand at the top of the cellar steps, while I get the coal?'

'Go on then Robert,' she would reply resignedly.

We had no electricity or hot water and certainly no such thing as torch. So I used to light a piece of rolled up newspaper, then our Mavis and I would stand at the top of the cellar steps peering down into the dark depths of the cellar. After a second or two of building up my courage I would set of at breakneck speed down the steps, throw the lighted newspaper on the floor, scoop up a shovelful of coal and run as fast as my little legs could carry me, back up the stairs to safety. And all the time, our faithful Mavis would be shouting at the top of her voice, 'Roberrrt! Roberrrt! Roberrrt!

I felt good, each time that once again I eluded the clutches of my imaginary monsters.

Now I know that some you readers may be wondering where the bathroom was? Well, we didn't have one! We had to get washed in the slop-stone sink. The toilet was about 100 yards away across a piece of land we called a common, and whenever we were taken short we had to do the 100 yard dash over the common hoping we could make it in time. The toilet was a decrepit old thing with the door falling off its hinges. Toilet paper was a luxury we couldn't afford so my mother used to cut pieces of newspaper and hang them on a piece of string behind the toilet door. I often wondered if we walked around with the headlines of the day imprinted on our bottoms. Maybe not, but a nice thought. The toilet seat was a long wooden board with a hole in it, and underneath was a tin for our waste. Every week some men from the council would come and empty it. Great job, eh! Can you imagine what happened in their houses in the morning?

Wife:	'Hurry up Love; you are going to be late for work.'
Council man:	'Nearly ready Love.'
Wife:	'So what are you doing today then?
Council man:	'Oh, getting rid of people's excrement.'
Wife:	'Oh that's different Love; I'll bet that's interesting.'

Council man: *'Well you know they say Love, where's*
               there's muck there's money.'
Wife: *'Aye, well have a nice day love; I'll have*
               some nice Finny Haddock for you when you
               get home.'

What a horrible job, I don't think I could have done that job for a million pounds a week. Now you won't believe this, but next door's toilet had a seat with two holes in it so that they could pass the time of day. That is true and to this day I have always found
the thought of that funny, because for the life in me I can't imagine anyone sitting there doing their No 2's chatting away to someone else. Anyway I feel it's time we changed the subject.

As I mentioned earlier, we had no electricity or hot water, so bath nights were a special event. My mother used to boil the kettles for hours on end to fill an old metal tub which, when not being used to bath us, would be stood in the middle of the stairs full of dirty clothes that needed washing. Bath night was usually twice a week, and if my mother had given clean water for each child, she would have been boiling kettles for weeks. So she would fill the tub once, and we would all have to use the same water. And guess who always got washed last? Me! And guess who my mother always seemed to wash the longest? Me! I hated bath nights. The water seemed so hot that I felt it was going to take my skin off. And to this day I can't take a hot bath. The water must be tepid. That's why I don't understand my wife. She can get in a hot bath that can only be described as torture, then she will put hot wax on her legs and pull the hair out by the roots, then she will pluck and shape her eye-brows, once again pulling the hair out by the roots, and yet she is still afraid of spiders. Anyway on bath night my mother would then rub some soap on a hard bristled scrubbing brush and then proceed to scrub us, hard. I use to wriggle and writhe, trying to get away from the bristles, but my mother always seemed to reach every nook and cranny of my body. I think she used to find some that weren't there.

'Keep still Robert,' she used to say. 'Cleanliness is next to godliness.'

I'll think my mother thought all her life that to be clean of body makes one closer to the Lord. What she wouldn't have realized was that your soul has to clean before you can get close to the Lord. The Lord can live in our spirit if we ask him too, but it is our soul

He wants to clean and no amount of scrubbing with a hard scrubbing brush was going to bring me closer to the Lord.

After nearly scrubbing me down to my bones, my mother would then proceed to wash my hair. But not for us the nice smelling shampoos that made you smell like you had been living in a flowered filled forest most of your life, oh no! We had good old fashioned Derbac soap. Guaranteed to kill all head lice! Yes, you read it right. Head lice. Just after the war it was very common to get head lice, or nits as we used to call them. Why they acquired that name, I will never know. Even when we went to school an inspector, usually a woman would come round checking the children's heads for lice. She was lovingly known as Nitty Norah the Nit Nurse.

After my mother had washed my hair in the nit-killing Derbac soap she would dry me off. And then I would have to kneel in front of her while she proceeded to go through my hair with an implement that I can only describe as belonging to a medieval torture chamber, the dreaded Derbac comb. It was designed to catch any nits that had managed to escape the acrid smell of the soap. It was a little steel comb with teeth so close together that none of the nits, or lice could escape. My mother used to pull the comb through my hair with such force that I felt she was in danger of breaking my neck. I often thought about it later but there must have been a salesman in England, going around selling these things.

'Roll up, roll up, don't forget to buy your Derbac soap, guaranteed to kill all nits, and if you buy two, you get a free Derbac comb.'

I have never met anyone yet who has admitting to selling them. And if I did I'm not sure they would admit it.

As I sit here, attempting to write this book, many thoughts and images from the past keep going through my mind. The old coconut matting we used to have, because my mother and father couldn't afford a proper carpet; my father always whistling and the sound of his clogs clumping on the pavement; the long hot summers we used to have; my sisters and I playing 'knock-a-door run-away'. Everything seemed so innocent then. My mother chasing the rag and bone man down the road, trying to exchange some rags for a piece of donkey-stone. A donkey-stone was a piece of crushed stone made into a block, and it was used to clean the front door step and the window-sills. In those by-gone days if someone had a dirty front step they were looked on as lazy. I can still my mother on her hands and knees scrubbing the front door step with her donkey-stone, and my father sitting on his stool talking to her.

Memories. Funny things, memories, I've got a million of them. And I wouldn't swop a single one, because even though there was hardship, I had a wonderful childhood, and I couldn't have asked for a more loving family. The only down-side I see to life now in the 21st century is that because of all the advancement in technology we seemed to have lost the simple things of life, but hey! Maybe that is because I am getting old.

My eldest sister, Sylvia, was a little older than Mavis and I and she had just discovered boys, so it was our Mavis and I who used to do everything together. We became inseparable. Wherever I went our Mavis was there. Whenever I played with my mates, our Mavis was there. Mind you, I was glad of this because she used to protect me; and if anybody was picking on me she would to beat them up. (Thanks, Mave. You were a right little tomboy).

Across the road from us lived the Waddington family, the parents were Frank and Alice, and they had two children who became our best friends, Frank junior, and Denise. Their father Frank was a farmer who used to deliver milk to all his customers around Shaw, and every Saturday morning I would rush out of the house just in time to see Old Frank going past in his milk float, with his old horse, Dobbin, pulling it.

'Come on, Bobby lad,' he would shout, 'come and help me to deliver the milk.'

And I would run as fast as my little legs could go until I caught them up, and then I would jump on the back of the milk float, fighting to get my breath. Old Frank would laugh and pat me on the back. Then he would let me take the reins. There I was, me, little Bobby Harper, in control of this huge beast. I felt I was the only boy in Shaw with this power. The old horse would slowly plod on, taking everything in its stride. But to me as a child that was the greatest horse in the world.

'Come on, Dobbin,' I would shout, and start making a clicking sound with my mouth. Boy! It felt good.

When we reached a row of houses Dobbin would stop and Old Frank would jump off the back with his bottles of milk and start to deliver them. Then Dobbin would set off again and stop at the next row of houses waiting for Old Frank to catch up. And there I was holding the reins controlling when Dobbin moved or stopped. Oh! The power, the control I had over this huge animal. Or so I thought I had. What I didn't realize until I was much older was that I didn't have any control over Dobbin at all. He had been going around the same streets and the same houses for many years that he automatically stopped and started on his own. And there was I, thinking that I was the one who was in control. What a Wally I was…Old Frank must have had many a little chuckle to himself.

I remember one Saturday morning our Mavis decided to join us; she ran with me and we both jumped up onto the back of the milk float. She wanted to hold the reins but I told her 'no way,' after all in my mind I was the only one that Dobbin would obey. The first place we had to deliver milk was at some cottages at the bottom of a very bumpy lane called the Button Hole. To call it a lane was being very generous; it was more or less a dirt track with lots of pot-holes in it. As we set off our Mavis was stood on a little step at the back of the milk, and for some reason that day she thought she was a princess. There she stood, posing , lost in her imaginary world thinking that the milk float was her chariot, when suddenly the cart hit a bump. Off she went, landing in the muddiest puddle in the lane. There she sat mud all over her, on her dress, in her lovely red hair; she was covered from head to toe. Suddenly from being a beautiful princess she had turned into a real life Cinderella. Old Frank hadn't noticed our Mavis fall off so he carried on as if nothing had happened. Children can be cruel, and I was no different. I started to laugh at her as we carried on down the lane. She started to cry. And then she ran home, never to be a princess again. To this day she has never forgotten that. She says that it wasn't the falling of the cart that hurt her. It was her friend and brother who left her sitting there (sorry Mave).

As far back as I can remember, my mother had always been a cotton worker and my father worked for a company that produced Asbestos. Looking back, my father had been very blessed not to have caught some sort of illness through working in the close proximity of asbestos in the way that he did. He had to travel quite a distance to work, and the bus that took him to work left at 6 a.m. so we all had to be up 5.30.a.m. My mother used to rouse us from our sleep and herd us downstairs like a shepherdess herding her sheep. Then she would make my fathers sandwiches for work, and then get us children ready for work. My father's sandwiches were always bread and beef dripping. The thought of it is enough to make me nauseous, but he loved them. He used to say they were good for you, he said the dripping used to stick to his ribs and it helped to keep the cold out. The people who lived around us used to say that my father was better than an alarm clock, because they could hear him coming by the sound of his clogs and his whistling.

After my mother had packed my father off to work she would start to get us dressed and herself ready for work. And on the cold dark winter mornings our Mavis and I would sit shivering and half asleep on the settee, waiting for our mother to dress us. Our Sylvia would dress herself, because she was already going to school and didn't need my mothers help.

One day a week we were allowed a comic between us, so on Tuesday mornings we had the Beano. Tuesday morning was the highlight of the week for us kids in our house. but if you think about it, with us only having one comic between three children there were the inevitable arguments, with our Sylvia saying she should have the comic first with he being the eldest; and our Mavis saying she should have it because she never got to read it first. And then there was me, who never argued but just looked at my mother, and giving her my best 'nobody loves me' look, could guarantee that nine times out of ten could get me the comic first.

Once I had the comic I would start to read it. And oh! The fantastic characters that used live in that comic. They would jump out of the pages and ignite my imagination, Desperate Dan, Korky the Kat. My sisters used to sit on the edge of the settee, waiting for me to finish. So

I would read slower, sometimes reading the same page twice. My sisters would start moaning to my mother,

'Mam, he's reading slow and he's doing it on purpose,' our Mavis would cry.

And our Sylvia would look at me, her eyes narrowing, full of venom.

'I'm going to kill you when my Mam's not looking if you don't hurry up!' she would whisper.

I would look at my mother for support and amongst all the arguing she would just look at me with all the patience in the world and say,

'Hurry up, Robert; I'm going to be later for work.'

Thinking back, my sisters were right, I was just wasting time.

My mother worked at the Lilac Mill. It was a huge cotton mill that dominated the village. It was the biggest of all the cotton mills in Shaw. It was very unusual as far as cotton mills go because it had its own ballroom on the top floor. I'm not talking a small ballroom but a huge ballroom with a polished floor and a stage that could hold a full orchestra. Around the perimeter of the dance floor there were wicker chairs and tables, so as you can imagine all this situated in a cotton mill, it was something that was unheard of in those days. For a cotton mill, it was very luxurious. The owners seemed to really care and provide for their workers, which was a rarity fifty years ago. The men and women used to start work at 7.30am and finish work at 5.30pm, with an hour break for lunch. Work in a cotton mill was gruelling and with the noise of the huge machinery, the drudge of repetition, plus the dust and grime, life was pretty hard. But at lunch time there was an escape from the reality of the cotton mill. The workers would all go up to the top floor to where the canteen was also situated, and if they hadn't brought their own lunch, they could choose from a variety of hot food which was provided. Without the noise of the machinery and the dust and grime the atmosphere in the canteen became very light-hearted. There was a hum of chatter with the men all sat together smoking their pipes and talking about football and darts and the women chatting away about babies and their dreams of the future.

The Lilac mill had a nurse on duty and a welfare officer named Mrs Wolsenholme. I really liked Mrs Wolsenholme, I think mainly because I was her favorite. Every lunch time she would play records for the workers in the ballroom, and after they had had their lunch they would go into the ballroom and dance for half an hour. Some of them would forego their lunches and dance for the full hour. It was strange to see. All these people laughing and dancing to the hit tunes of the day, Glenn Miller, Doris Day and many others, and just a floor below was the starkness of reality, but here lay escapism. One Saturday in every month she would hold a dance and all the workers with their families would arrive in their best clothes to dance the night away. I remember going to quite a few of them. It was great fun as a child, skidding around the dance floor, pretending to dance like adults, and being able to get away from the watchful eyes of my parents for a few minutes.

They even had a nursery where young mothers could bring their children to be looked after by registered child minders while they went and did a hard days work. This was the place that my mother took us and it was a place that molded my life. I remember the winters were particularly hard. After my mother had got my dad off to work and got us all ready we would set off for the nursery. We would leave home about 6.30 in the morning while it was still dark. We would make our way down Button Hole Lane, through some fields and over a hill named the Haydings. The cold harsh wind would blow through our thin clothes and I would always start to shiver. I hated those winter mornings. Sometimes my mother would pick me up and I would snuggle deep into her, and it felt good to feel the warmth of my mother. I would try to bury myself under her clothes, away from the cold winter wind. My poor mother, just imagine it; a little woman in her old coat and head scarf having to walk three of four miles carrying a small child, with two other children hanging onto her coat, battling against the elements of winter. Every now and again she would put her tiny hand around one of my sisters, as if to give them reassurance. That was my mother. She stood only four foot ten, but she had an inner strength that made up for her lack of inches.

I remember a story that my mother used to tell us. I was only a baby at the time, and with us living up on the moorland when winter arrived, we always seemed to get the worst of the snow. That particular year, 1947 to be exact was a particular bad winter and we had no coal to keep us warm. So my mother told us to stay in bed while she went to get some coal. My mother's best friend was a woman named Elsie Henthorn, whose family was as poor as ours. This particular day, according to my mothers story, they had got their respective husbands off to work and together they decided they would walk the three or four miles over the moor to an old disused coal-pit to see if they could find any loose coal lying around the pit entrance. So these two women set off across the bleak snow-bound moors, dragging behind them two sledges on which they could put the coal they were hoping to find. Finally after battling the elements they reached coal pit entrance, and to their joy they found lots of small pieces of coal lying around. They loaded up their sledges and set off for home across the moors with their black treasure. You can imagine the joy in their hearts as they battled through the deep snow. They would have been chatting about they could now get the houses warm for when their husbands arrived home for work, and how they could get their kids warm. They must have been excited and satisfied. When they got about a mile

25

from our house, the string attached to my mother's sledge snapped, and all the coal she had collected went tumbling down the hill. My mother said she just sat in the snow and cried her heart out. I can't remember whether she managed to bring any coal home or not, but it didn't matter, because of my mother's love we survived.

In 1984 I was walking through Shaw and I happened to look in a photographer's window, and I was astonished. Unbelievably there was a picture from 1947 of my mother and Elsie Henthorn pushing a pram up the hill through the snow. I immediately bought the picture and gave it to my mother. She kept that photograph was on my mother's wall until the day she died. Sadly the picture has been lost, but it still remains in my memory.

At the nursery I had already become a little star. I was about two or three years of age at the time, and the radio had a weekly programme named *Worker's Playtime*. The program used to visit different factories in different towns each week and put a show on for the workers of the chosen factories. Well, they finally decided to come to Shaw and record their program at the Lilac mill. Mrs. Wolsenholme must have told them about this little boy who couldn't stop telling nursery rhymes and singing. So they asked me if I would do something for them. Would I? There was no stopping me. I was a proper little show-off. Anyway after a lot of persuasion (about a second) I decided to recite a little poem my father had taught me: 'I had a little pony'.

> I had a little pony
> It was a dapple grey
> I lent it to a lady
> Who rode it far away
> She whipped it, and she lashed it
> She rode it through the mire
> I would not lend my pony again
> For all my hearts desire

That's the poem I recited on radio, and it was my first introduction to the world of show-biz.

Another time I was playing in the nursery when I decided I was going to be Superman. I got my coat and tied it around the back of neck so that to my mind it looked like a cloak. My grandchildren have all done the same at some stage. I felt I was and looked like Superman. Of course, I most probably looked like some kid with a coat tied to his neck, but it didn't matter in my mind I was Superman. I arranged a pile of cushions and proceeded to climb to the top of this gate and with a shout of 'SHAZZAM' (That is what I thought Superman used to shout), I dived off, heading for the pile of cushions not far away. Yes, that's right. I wasn't Superman and I couldn't fly. Down I went like a lead balloon, missing the cushions. Crash! My head bounced off the floor like a basketball in the hands of a Harlem Globetrotter. I had a few bumps, but worst of all I had bitten my tongue and it was hanging off. The nurse let my mother know what had happened and then they rushed me off to the hospital. I didn't really know what was happening but apparently they sewed my tongue back together. They told my mother that she had to take me back the following week to see how my tongue was healing. A week later my mother took me back and she was quite panic-stricken.

'Doctor,' she said 'I think our Robert has swallowed his stitches.'

The doctor looked at my mother as if she had gone mad, but then realized what she was talking about.

'Mrs Harper,' he said, with a smile on his face, 'your Robert hasn't swallowed his stitches.'

'But he has,' replied, more adamant than ever, 'I looked at his tongue last night and his stitches have disappeared.'

'I know,' the doctor said, 'they will have because we used dissolving stitches.'

'Oh, I see,' replied my mother, she was very embarrassed.

And with that knowledge she quickly put my coat on and took me home. But to this day I am convinced that my mother still thought that I had swallowed my stitches.

Every year Mrs. Wolsenholme would put together a children's concert for the workers at lunchtime. It was always a big event with lavish costumes which Mrs. Wolsenholme had faithfully spent all year making. We even wore stage make-up and had a band. Mrs. Wolsenholme would have us rehearse regularly during the days prior to the concert and as the day approached the atmosphere got quite intense. This particular year I had to sing a song entitled, 'I'm the rich Maharaja from Matador'. So I had to wear these baggy trousers, pointed shoes and a turban. I also had to wear dark make-up, covering my face and body, to make me look like a Maharaja. Our poor Mavis was a harem girl. She had to stand behind me through the whole song, fanning me the whole time with a huge cardboard fan. For about three days before the concert, like the Prima Donna that I am, I kept telling our Mavis that she wasn't fanning me the right way,

'You're fanning me too fast, Mave,' I would say, or, 'You're fanning me too slow.'

All this nagging her was slowly bringing her patience threshold down to as low as it could go, and finally on the morning of the concert she snapped.

'You're not doing it right, Mave,' I said once again.

Suddenly I heard this almighty crash and something hit me on the head. It was the cardboard fan. There I was with my turban flattened and a broken cardboard fan hanging around my shoulders.

'I'm not doing this anymore,' screamed our Mavis, and ran off in a huff.

Needless to say good old Mrs. Wolsenhome calmed

everything down and our Mavis went on to become a huge success as the fan carrier. But Mavis, if you are reading this book, I still reckon you were fanning too fast.

One morning my mother took us to the nursery and there was a lot of commotion going on. We were being moved to a purpose-built nursery that had been built in the grounds of the Lilac mill. It was a beautiful place with all the modern facilities for looking after children. We also had two new nannies, Nanny Smith and Nanny Barlow. Nanny Barlow was my favorite. She was a lovely old lady with white hair and kind eyes. Nothing was too much trouble for her. She never seemed to lose her temper with the children and she seemed to take a special interest in our Mavis and me, I think it's because we were the poorest. I continued to visit her till I was well into my teens. And I still called her Nanny Barlow until the day she died.

Around 1952 we were told that the Queen was to officially open the nursery, and all the workers were given a day's holiday. It was the biggest day that had ever happened in Shaw. (Apart from when I was born, just kidding.) All the children from the nursery had to stand in a line in the nursery grounds, and when she arrived we all had to wave these little Union Jack flags that we had been given. To tell you the truth I was more interested in keeping the flag than seeing this person that everybody was making a fuss about. We had many days practicing waving our flags and when the arrived and we all stood in a line. Suddenly she arrived. I was expecting to see a Queen with a crown on her head and wearing robes, but all I saw was this young lady wearing an ordinary coat and fancy hat on her head. But I didn't let my disappointment dampen my enthusiasm. As soon as she came though the gate we all shouted, 'Hurrah, hurrah.' With me shouting the loudest, wanting to be noticed. With all these people gathered around her she

29

seemed so graceful and important that to me she seemed like the most important nanny in the world. 'Hurrah,' I shouted even louder. She slowly came along the line, every now and again stopping to talk to the children. She's bound to stop and talk to me; I thought to myself, after all, I've just played the starring role as the Maharaja of Matador in the nursery's concert. But no, she walked straight past me. I was bitterly disappointed. I did meet her later on in my life, and she spoke to me then.

Nursery life was great, but there was one great drawback, the castor oil! It happened once a week and we would have to stand in a line, with Nanny Barlow at one end talking nicely to us and Nanny Smith at the other end dishing out the castor oil. I would stand there hoping against hope that I would never reach the front of the line. But eventually I would be there, looking up at Nanny Smith, who in turn would be looking down at me with a huge spoonful of castor oil. I am sure that sometimes I saw a sadistic smile float across her mouth. I would screw up my face and gulp it down as quickly as I could, hoping that none of the wretched stuff would touch the insides of my mouth. Then came the nice bit, she would then dip another spoon into a huge can of black malt treacle. It was so thick that I am sure it could have been used to damp-proof a flat roof. But I loved it. I used to let it linger in my mouth and savor the taste. Oh, I can taste it now.

So that's what it was like at nursery when I was a child. And the friends I made at nursery were still the same friends right into my teenage years. The Two friends I fondly remember were Dennis and Glenys Henthorn, who were twins, and they didn't live far from us on the moors. Dennis was my closest friend all through my childhood. He was a very robust child with wild blonde curly hair and a laughing face. Sometimes when I am alone my memory wanders back to those days, and I wonder where Dennis and Glenys are now? What are they doing? It's sad sometimes how through our walk in life we let friends just drift away.

Dennis and I had many adventures together. I remember one adventure we had with clarity because I didn't suffer because of it until thirty years later. Dennis and I had decided to go and play in the fields surrounding our houses, so my mother warned us in no un-certain terms not to go near the Clough mill lodge. This was a vast volume of water that was used to cool down the steam system in the mill. And, because we were told not to go near it, Dennis and I, as children do, decided to go play at the lodge. When we reached the lodge we decided to play boats, so we got two twigs and proceeded to float them in the water. As luck would have it, my twig, or my boat as it was to me, began to float away from the edge and, me being a typical boy, thoughtlessly leaned over to try to get it back. And plop! Before I knew where I was, I was in the freezing water and going down. Now, at this point I couldn't swim so you could say that I was in a bit of trouble. I remember I kept coming up and gasping for air and seeing Dennis's face looking at me from the bank. Inside I was panicking and the more I panicked, the more I seemed to go under the water. Suddenly Dennis's hand came out and grabbed my hair and before I knew where I was, he was hauling me up onto the bank. There I lay coughing and spluttering and feeling like a drowned rat. I had really panicked. After a while I had composed myself and sat there shivering, reliving my ordeal. Then Dennis reminded about the dilemma that we were in. We couldn't tell our mothers what had happened because they had told us to stay away from the mill lodge. So we came upon a master plan. We decided to see if we could dry my clothes and then go home as if nothing had happened. I took my clothes off and hung them on a tree and stood there as naked as the day I was born. I was absolutely freezing. Even my goose-pimples had goose-pimples. It was a very overcast day that day with a cold wind blowing down from the moors. But with our childish optimism we thought that we would have no trouble drying my clothes. After about an hour of watching my clothes not getting any drier we decided to tell our mothers a story that would get us out of trouble. I put my wet clothes back on and Dennis and I got down to plotting. We decided to tell them that we had gone for a walk and met some big lads who had thrown me in a river and Dennis had saved my life, which in essence he had done, only there were no other boys and no river. There had just been me and him, trying to sail a boat in a place where I shouldn't have been. But yes, it was a good story and we decided that it was the one which would save our bacon. We set off for home with this lie firmly planted in our brains. When we reached home and walked through the front door my mother threw her arms up in the air.

'Oh no' she shrieked 'Whatever has happened?

She stood there looking at her son as if I had been the only survivor from the Titanic.

Dennis proceeded to tell her our story and I just stood there in my wet clothes trying to look as sorrowful as I could manage. My mother looked at Dennis then at me. For a moment fear rushed through my body thinking that maybe just maybe my mother had seen through our lies. Suddenly she gave Dennis a big hug.

'You've been a very good boy, Dennis,' she said. 'You have saved our Robert's life.'

When she had finished praising Dennis she opened her purse and gave him a shilling. We couldn't believe it. We had got away with it. Dennis thanked my mother for the money and left and I got pampered for the rest of the day. Dennis and I spent the money the next day on sweets and stuff. Thirty years later when I about thirty six years of age I told my mother the truth, thinking it was great laugh. Much to my surprise she suddenly hit me across the head.

'What's that for Mam? I said, completely surprised.

'That,' she said 'is because that shilling I gave Dennis was the only money I had in purse and not only that you got that slap for telling lies. It just shows that you pay the consequences no matter how long it takes.

There are many other faces that wander through my memory. One is of Billy Lupton, who was the nursery bully for a time. Everyone was frightened of him, even our Mave. He was bigger than any of us and he would continually batter and intimidate us. But for him it must have been a childhood thing because as he got older he changed and became one of the nicest men anyone could wish to meet. I remember once when we were both grown up we went fishing and had some great laughs, remembering the old times. Sadly Billy passed away but I am glad that I got to know the real Billy Lupton, a kind and gentle man.

Then there was Dennis Cockcroft, a big lad with a voice that seemed totally alien to his size. He had a wonderful soprano voice. When he sang it was like you would imagine angels sang. He would be asked to sing at the nursery so he and I would compete to see who the best singer was. Looking back he seemed destined to be one of our great classical singers but sadly when he reached about fourteen years of age his voice broke and he could no longer hit the notes he could so that was the end of his singing career. Luckily for me I have always had a low type of voice so even though my voice broke, like everyone's does, I didn't notice it so I just carried on being a little show-off.

It was at the nursery that I also met my first love. Ann Sheriff, a little girl with black hair and laughing eyes. The thing I liked most about her was that she always wore nice, smart clothes. Isn't it funny how things like that stick in children's minds. I thought she was wonderful, and used to look forward to going to the nursery to see her. She was to me what dreams were made on. I used to give her my gobstopper toffee, but it was to no avail, my loving overtures were not reciprocated. In other words she didn't like me. If I had only known then what I know now, I wouldn't have given her my precious gobstopper. You see, no girl to a six year old boy was worth a gobstopper, least of all one that didn't like me.

Then there was our Jack, my cousin. Jack didn't live far from us, so we had our own little gang that played together all the time. There was Frank Waddington Jnr. and his sister Denise, Dennis and Glenys Henthorn, our Jack and me. Oh, and I mustn't forget our Mavis.

I remember quite vividly the winter of 1949. I was five years old and it was one of the worst winters Britain had ever seen. Well, according to what the adults said. Up on the moors where we lived the snow had drifted to twenty feet deep, and the landscape looked bleak and desolate. But in a strange way it was beautiful. It was absolutely freezing, so my mother had to put more coats on the beds. We didn't have blankets so she used to buy old clothes from the jumble sales and put them on the beds to keep us warm. I had an old army coat on my bed and I used to wonder a lot about that coat, who had worn it? Is he dead or alive? What was he like? Well whoever he was I'll bet he never have guessed that the coat that had kept him warm in the war was now keeping a little boy warm high up on the Pennine moors. My mother tried her best to keep us warm, but the cold didn't bother us kids, we were too busy having a great time in the snow. My father had made us a sledge and it was the best one I had ever seen. So with my new sledge and the snow so high I felt like I was some intrepid explorer about to start out on his latest adventure. In actual fact I was, and the goal was the steepest hill in all of Shaw. The gang and I would take our sledges to the top of a hill called the Roses Brew and sledge all the way down. It was a run of about five hundred yards. When we reached the bottom we would have to walk, dragging our sledges, all the way back up to the top. It seem to take ages walking back up to the top, but it was worth for the minute of pleasure we got sledging down. On the way back to the top of Roses Brew, snow would collect on the bottom of our clogs and we called these cloggy-bobs. The snow on our clogs would make us about two or three inches taller. And it was great fun trying to walk, because the snow on our clogs would make us slip more. But woe betide any of us who didn't knock the snow off before we arrived home. Our mothers would hit the roof with us for walking all the snow into the house.

The weekends were always a special time for me. My mother and father weren't working so we did everything together as a family. Friday evening my father would come home from work, have his tea, and if any coal had been delivered we would all carry it down into the dreaded dark cellar in buckets. Strange but my fear of monsters would always seem to disappear when my dad was there. And when we weren't doing that, we would be some other job. Then when all the chores had been done, my father would get washed. I can see him now standing in front of the slop-stone sink washing himself in the freezing water. Then he would change into his weekend clothes, put on his flat cap and his clogs, give us all a kiss and off he would go to the pub. We were able to hear him whistling as he walked off into the distance. The fire would be burning heartily and my mother would finish all her chores and she would wearily sit down in an old armchair. We had no television then, so my mother would say, 'Let's have a concert.' Our Mavis and I would get very excited and we would proceed to entertain her by putting on one our little shows. About ten thirty we would hear my father coming down the road, whistling as usual. We would jump into the ovens at the side of the fireplace, and wait for him to come through the door. As he came in he would hang his cap on a special nail behind the door and give us all a big smile. I can still see the look of pride on his face as he looked at his family. It was a very exciting time for us because we knew that he would start to tell us fascinating stories about when he was a child and growing and that meant we could get to stay up longer.

Every time my father went to the pub without my mother he would bring back home a bottle of Mackeson's stout beer for her. It was a thick, dark beer and my mother loved it. It became a kind of ritual between my mother and father. He would pour her stout into a glass and then put a poker into the fire until it was glowing red hot, then he would put the poker into the glass of stout. I would watch the black stout, fascinated as it fizzled and frothed, trying to fight the heat of the poker. Then my mother would drink the stout (without the poker in it, I hasten to add). My father used to say it was best drink anyone could take, because when the poker went into the stout small pieces of iron would disintegrate into the stout, making it a drink that was good for the blood. I never fully understood that when I was a boy, but as I grew older I could see what my father meant. My mother was anemic, you see, so my father was giving her the equivalent of today's iron tablets that are used for people with a deficiency in the blood. My Father had many remedies like that.

After my mother had drunk her iron stout, my father would sit me on his knee and begin his stories of when he was a boy. The stories he used to tell me were fascinating. His grandmother and the generations before her were traveling people. He said they were Romanizes. They worked on fairgrounds and traveled from place to place in their caravans. The fairgrounds in those days sounded much more exciting then the fair-grounds today and it was such a special event when they came to town. There was much more entertainment then because the fairgrounds had side-shows, with bearded ladies, strong men, fakirs and all sorts of wonderful things.

According to my father, my great- grandfather worked in the boxing booth and my great- grandmother worked in one of the side shows as a snake charmer, and apparently was a great draw. My father used to tell us one story about her, that one day she bought a new snake, a boa constrictor, apparently a huge beast. She had hardly worked with the snake and one night she decided to put it in her act. She proceeded to put the snake around her. Life in those days was much more simple and naive so the audience must have been spellbound to see this woman with a huge snake wrapped around her. Anyway something must have frightened the snake, because it started to constrict its body and began to suffocate her. Thankfully for her, the riggers who used to put up the tents, saw what was happening saw what was happening and ran as fast as they could to help. One of them pulled out his knife and slit the snake in two. As a boy that story was guaranteed to get my imaginative juices flowing. I never knew what happened to my great-grandmother after that, but she would have most likely lived to see another day and charmed another snake. But she will always be in my memory as the woman who escaped the boa constrictor.

Those evenings sitting around the fire listening to our parents telling us stories were unforgettable. We may have been a poor family, but if love was money then we were multi-millionaires.

Saturday night was the best night of the week for me. It was club night. My mother and father would get us dressed up as best they could and take us down to the Shaw Labour Club. The club was situated in the centre of Shaw, and with my father being a Labour supporter, he thought of it as his club. It had a concert room where the parents could sit and have a drink whilst watching a visiting artiste who would come to the club every week-end to entertain them. It also had a smaller room for the children to play in. We were not allowed in the concert room because they served alcohol, but we weren't particularly bothered, we had a great time running up and down the stairs. Occasionally they would break the rules and ask my father if I could sing for them. My father would come and collect me from the children's room and take me into the big concert room. I felt very special. There I was, this little boy, standing on a big stage in front of all these adults. And you know something? I absolutely loved it. I felt as if I belonged here. The microphone was too tall for me, so I had to stand on a stool to reach. It was very precarious. But it didn't matter, that was the last thing on my mind. All I could think about was singing. I sang my song and the crowd went crazy (I can't help being so modest. I will have to start taking my confidence pills). Another night when they asked me to sing, the pianist Eric Barlow, started to play the introduction to the song I was going to sing. But when it came my time to sing I found I couldn't find the pitch of the song. Eric stopped playing and looked at me.

'What's the problem, Bobby?' he asked.

I just looked at him with a vacant stare.

'It must be in the wrong key,' he said, and started to play the song again. Suddenly I stopped him.

'No! No! Mr. Barlow,' I said, 'that's not right.'

He stopped playing and just looked at me. He must have thought I was so precocious. Now he had a vacant look on his face.

'This is the key,' I said, getting down from my stool, and I hit one of the keys on the piano.

Like an automaton, Eric started to play. Unknown to him, I hadn't a clue which key was which, I just hit one, but you know, it was the right key. He just looked at me in disbelief. He must have thought I was a child genius. After that night I'll bet that Eric Barlow would have lived the rest of his life thinking that little Bobby Harper was a wonder child.

On the way home from the club my father and I used to have races. He always let me win, but I always thought I had won on merit. Isn't it great how some parents just naturally know how to build a child's self esteem? I remember one night my father and I were having our usual race with me in front winning, when I turned around to see how far my father was behind me. As I looked I saw my father in a crumpled heap on the floor. He had fallen. He pretended not to be hurt but I could see by the pained expression on his face that he was. I had no idea at the time, being a child, that this was the start of his life long battle against arthritis. It was sad to watch how this horrendous ailment could bring this great sportsman down to a crippled wreck.

Our Mavis and I would sing together at home, so she eventually joined me on stage and we became good enough to be asked to sing every Saturday night at the club. Occasionally we would miss going to the Labour club and my mother and father would take us to other clubs in the area. People had heard about our Mavis and me so they asked to perform at their local clubs. One night, when I was about six years of age my parents took us to the High Crompton Conservative Club, which was situated about a mile out of Shaw. It was the posh end of town. About half way through the night the committee asked my father if he would let me got up on stage and sing. My father agreed and I got on to the stage, confident as usual, and proceeded to sing my little heart out, loving every minute of it. In the club that night was a stranger, everybody could tell he was a stranger because he was wearing a trilby hat and everybody then wore flat caps, but I think that the real clue that gave him away as a stranger was that he had a cockney accent. When I had finished singing he came over to our table and asked my father if he would mind stepping outside with him for a minute. My father thought the fellow wanted to fight, so he put on his macho voice and said, 'No

problem,' and followed him out. When they got outside
the man asked my father if he would mind sitting in his
car as he wanted to talk with him. There were very few
cars in Shaw in those days and anyone who owned one
must obviously be very wealthy, my father was
impressed. They sat in the car and he said he would like
to be my manager. This was all new to my father, so he
had to explain what he meant. The man said he would
like to take me to London as he had a song he would like
me to record, and he would put me in stage school as he
thought I had potential. He wanted to groom me to be a
star. He offered my father five-hundred pounds. He was
astounded. In those days five-hundred was like offering
five-thousand. My father told the man that no amount of
money could buy his son, and that I would stay right
where I belonged, with my family. The man said he
understood and gave him five-pounds. He told my
father that it was for me to have singing lessons.

Needless to say I never had the singing lessons,
because the very next day my mother took the three of us
down to the Co-op clothing store and bought us all new
clothes. It was the first time we had been bought new
clothes and they felt and smelled wonderful. I had new
Wellingtons which were brown and yellow with a gold
sheriffs' star on either side. I also got a new raincoat, but
that wasn't as great as the wellies. Our Mavis was over
the moon because she finally got her first pair of new
shoes. And our Sylvia sulked because she wanted a blue
raincoat instead of a grey one. Walking back home that
day we all felt very posh indeed. There I was jumping in
every puddle I could find and Mavis almost walking on
tiptoe so she wouldn't ruin her new shoes. Sylvia carried
on sulking; she claimed that young ladies did not wear
grey. That is a memory that will never leave me. When
my father came home, we all paraded in front of him in
our new clothes. He then asked Mavis for her new shoes
and put pieces of cardboard in them. He said it would

save the sole. To this day I've never understood the logic of that.

One day Denise Waddington came across the common to our house very excited. They had a new television, she told us. To us they seemed to have the world, they had electricity, and we only had gaslight, and now they had a telly. I thought Denise was the luckiest girl in the world. They invited us across to watch it that night. I remember sitting between old Frank Waddington's legs and watching a program called 'The Quatermass Experiment.' It was a science fiction play about a man who had come back from a mission to Mars and picked up a deadly disease. One day in the laboratory he touched a cactus and slowly his whole body turned into a killing cactus. It nearly frightened me to death. Later that night, when it was time to go home, we had to cross the dark common and we ran as fast as we could, thinking that the killer cactus was behind us. For years after I couldn't go past a tree without thinking that maybe it would come to life any second.

We had many happy years up on the moors. Summertime would find us going for long walks and my father used to make us take old milk bottles with us and if we saw a stream and the grass beside it had turned brown, he would make us fill the milk bottles. He said this was natural iron water and was good for the stomach. He had lots of remedies like this; I think they had been passed down from his Romany ancestors. I remember once that my mother had a growth on her thumb, it grew and before long it covered her whole thumb. She was given some cream by the local village doctor and she applied it for about a week. It didn't do any good. By this time she had stopped cooking because her thumb was so infected and she was frightened of contaminating the food. My father then stepped in. He told us children to go into the fields and collect as many dandelion flowers as we could, which we did. We came back with thousands of them, and gave them to my father who was sitting in the kitchen with my mother. We watched as he split the stems and ran the juices from inside the stalks onto my mothers thumb. And within a couple of days the growth had began to go down, within a week it had disappeared altogether.

As a child I accepted this as normal but when I grew older I realized that my father knew more about natural medicines than I gave him credit for. I am sure that in the world around us there are natural remedies to fight many diseases.

By the year of 1949 I had reached the grand age of five. It was time for me to go to primary school. Like my two sisters, my mother sent me to the Shaw Wesleyan School. What she didn't know, or maybe she did, was that all my mates, such as Dennis Henthorne and our Jack, had been sent to the East Crompton School. I remember my first day. Our Mavis held my hand and led me there. Our Sylvia had already moved up to the Crompton House Senior School. Our Mavis walked me into the playground and stood with me until it was time to go to her class. I was then left with a load of first day children. I felt so alone, just standing there waiting for the unknown. Finally a teacher gathered us all together and herded us into a classroom. I sat there at this desk wondering what had happened to our Mavis. I knew deep inside that this wasn't the place for me. The kids at the school seemed different from the kids at the East Crompton School. Here, the children seemed very rich. After all, they had indoor toilets, electricity and they had school uniforms. My mother had to get ours on tick.

After school our Mavis and I would have to go to the nursery and wait for my mother to finish work. On the way to the nursery we would stop at the River Beal and fish for sticklebacks with worms. When I caught one I couldn't take the fish off the worm so I just used let it dangle in the water.

Eventually, with our Mavis being a couple of years older than me, she left our school and went up to the senior school. This left me really alone. By now I got used to feeling inferior to the others and besides, I could fight them all. So our Mavis' leaving was not too bad.

One Thursday afternoon there was a lot of excitement among the children at school. Friday was the day that 'The Topper' comic came out, and this week there was a free gift with every copy. The free gift was a toy called a Banger. It consisted of two pieces of cardboard with a piece of brown paper stuck between them. When you whizzed it through the air, it made a banging sound. Friday morning arrived and I begged my mother for 3d, which I doubt she could afford. As soon as I had the money I ran all the way down to Mr. Parkinson's paper shop, which was conveniently situated at the side of the school.

"Could I have the Topper please, Mr. Parkinson?" I asked eager to get my hands on the Banger.

"I'm, sorry Bobby," he replied, "we have sold out"

My little heart sank. My disappointment was so huge that I thought I was going to burst into tears.

"I'll have the 'Beano' then", I said quietly, trying not to cry.

When I got into the school yard it seemed all the other kids had their Bangers.

"Harper! Where's your Banger?" they all kept asking, but I told them that I didn't want the Topper, but that I really liked the Beano instead. Inside I was as sick as a parrot!

Another evening around that time, which I particularly remember was when I was literally 'tarred and feathered'. It happened when school was over and I was on my way to the nursery to wait for my mother. She had just gone into debt to buy me some new clothes for school and that day was the first day that I was wearing them. It was the middle of summer and really hot. So I

43

took my time, (dawdling, my mother used to call it) getting to the nursery. Suddenly I came across a huge mound of tarmac at the side of the road. A child's delight if ever there was one. I decided to see if I could run up it in one go. So I set off and made it, I got to the top in one go. What I didn't realize was that the heat had melted the centre of the tarmac so when I reached the top, slop! I sank into the middle. It was terrifying, I don't know how I managed to get out but I did. I was covered from head to foot in tar. It was everywhere, all over my clothes, my head, and my hair, everywhere. I started to cry. If ever I needed my mother it was now. I tried to run but couldn't, so I walked. I trudged along as though I had two broken legs. By now I had progressed from crying into a state of bawling. Everyone stared as I made my way to the cotton mill where my mother worked. I knew that when I found her she would put everything right. The walk seemed twice as long and when I reached the mill I found the big room where my mother worked. The noise was deafening, it was so loud that I felt lost among it all. My mother was nowhere to be seen. As I searched, people began to stop what they were doing to stop and stare at me. I was such a sight; I had turned completely black from head to foot and was walking as though I had done something nasty in my trousers. I looked around; not realizing that all the little bits of cotton flying about in the room had began to settle on me. And then I saw her. She was staring from across the room with her mouth wide open in disbelief. This made me bawl even louder. I began to make my way towards her, but the more I moved the more the cotton stuck to me. When I did eventually reach her I was truly tarred and cottoned.

My mother just stood there staring at me not believing what she was seeing, I gave her my most pitiful look and wondered how long I would have to stand there before she made everything alright. Suddenly she gave me such a clip around the ear; I thought I wouldn't hear for a week. I bawled even more. I was now wailing louder than the machinery. She shouted at me for ruining my clothes that hadn't even been paid for yet and marched me home. I don't know what happened after that but for the next few years, whenever I saw a tarmac mound; I gave it an extremely wide berth.

Now I was safely settled into school, my mother allowed me to go to the 3d matinee with our Mavis. This was the Saturday afternoon performance at the local cinema, The Princess. We called it the 'Prinnie,' it cost us 3d entrance fee. I used to wait eagerly all week for Saturdays and when it arrived our Mavis and I would run all the way down to the cinema and wait outside with the other kids. The doors would open and we would all dash in together madly as though they were going to close the doors at any minute. There was no parental guidance at the 3d matinee, so you can imagine what it was like, five-hundred children screaming and flicking bits of paper at the screen. It was total bedlam. Thankfully for the staff, we all managed to calm down when the picture started.

They always ran a short film first which was usually Flash Gordon. It had everything for children, a villain, 'Emperor Ming,' and a 'goodie,' 'Count Zarcoff of the bird people'. He would parade about with two huge wings strapped to his back. Flash was the hero. The sci-fi program was on every week and each time Flash would be left in yet another dangerous situation. For instance, the spaceship with Flash inside would blow up and suddenly a deep American voice would boom out, 'Is Flash dead, killed by a bomb planted on his ship by Emperor Ming? Find out next week.' And there we were, left hanging by this remark, all sitting wide eyed and open mouthed, wondering if they would ever see Flash Gordon again. But sure enough the next week he would reappear, and jump out of his spaceship or whatever peril had been in his way before it blew up. Marvelous stuff.

When the main film came on, usually a western, cowboy one with great names like Hopalong Cassidy or Lash Larue, we would all cheer or boo as the 'goodies and baddies' appeared on screen. We could always who was who from the color of their hats; the hat the hero wore would always be white whereas the villain would be in black. When the film was over the kids would all hurry out of the cinema, re-enacting what we had just seen. I was no exception. Off up to the moors I would run, clicking my tongue to make the sound of the horses' hooves, pretending to be Black Bart, scourge of the West. Our Mavis would be running up behind me, usually in a sulk because I'd cast her as 'Sitting Bull', she'd always say she didn't want to be an Indian, who were then unfairly cast as the enemy, but nine times out of ten, that's who she would end up as. (And if you don't mind my saying so, Mavis, you were a very good Indian).

My life suddenly changed when I was ten years old. It was 1954 when a man arrived from the local council to inform my parents that we could at last have a council house. We were so excited. The mood in our house that night was overwhelming joy. They had even given us a choice. We could go to a local estate or move into one of a few which the council owned at the end of George Street. My parents decided on the George Street house, because, my father said, 'It's been built with proper bricks.' Obviously, I didn't understand him at all.

After my parents had made their choice known to the council officer, he told them that everything was in order and we could move into it in a weeks' time, no long waiting lists in those days. There was no such thing as 'red tape'. The week flew by in a blur and on the day of the move my father hired a wagon from Cuss the Coalman to transport our few belongings down to the new house. They piled up the beds, the sideboard and all our bits and pieces. My mother had our old pram and anything that wouldn't fit on the wagon, or she whatever she didn't trust to make it there in one piece, we put into it. I remember my mother, Sylvia, Mavis and myself all pushing this heavy pram down to George Street. It was about a quarter of a mile long, but to me it was the longest street in the world. It was just one street, with a row of a few houses, surrounded by fields. There was a huge oak tree nearby, which I loved; it was so tall and majestic standing there. A few years later, after I was married and moved away from my parents' house, the developers uprooted it and built an estate where it had stood, I never understood why they couldn't just build the houses around my beloved oak tree, and still wonder why man destroys natural beauty and replaces it with ugliness.

When we reached our new house, it was like some kind of palace to me. I now had what all my friends took for granted. There was a garden both front and back and *three* bedrooms! And, how's this for posh, we had a front door and a back door! There was also a flushing outside toilet. But the biggest and best luxury of all was electricity and hot water. I felt we had moved up in the world. It all became too much for my mother because from the moment we entered, I began switching the lights on and off obsessively, they fascinated me. My mother gave me a slap and ordered me to stop because; she said 'the Germans will think we're signaling'. The war had been over nine years! The daftest thing was I believed her.

We had become respectable, and now that we had electricity, my father bought us a television. We were so excited. Nowadays we take them for granted, and they seem to be in every room, let alone every home, but to us then it was one of the biggest things that could happen in our lives. They used to finish broadcasting at ten thirty, but we even stayed up to watch the dot disappear. It was fantastic.

For me the age of ten was a turning point, I was about to go up to the big school and enter a whole new world. There I would discover two things that would change my life forever.

Chapter 2

Brylcreem &
Brothel-Creepers

In 1955, my life changed dramatically when I began at Crompton House Senior School. Our Sylvia by this time had left and was already married, so there was only our Mavis there to see me through my first day. I had heard that the first year students had to go through some kind of initiation ceremony and I was very nervous.

Crompton House was, and still is, a very imposing structure. It looks like an old mansion which has been turned into a school, with gothic features and large mullioned windows. Inside it had long corridors and staircases which seemed to just go up and up. I imagine it wouldn't be out of place in a Bronte novel. It was very overwhelming to me at eleven years old.

When the day arrived for me to go I felt as though I was going on an adventure. My mother made the minimum of fuss and handed my lunch money over before she left for work. She instructed me to listen to our Mavis but I wasn't going to do that! I was eleven years old and could take care of myself just fine. Mavis and I set off for the bus at eight-fifteen. The bus was a single deck, with no number, but a letter, F. We called it the little F.

When I got off the bus outside the school, I was a little awestruck. I just stood there staring at this huge old school, and suddenly felt very small. I was stepping into the unknown. My head was swimming. I still had a feeling that I didn't belong, which remained with me until one day when something happened to make things very different indeed.

Our Mavis and I had to separate. The girls' and boys' playgrounds were two distinct areas and we couldn't mix. I fearfully and very hesitantly made my way to the huge iron gates which led to the boys' playground. I knew what was coming, I was about to be initiated.

Let me explain about the initiation, it was named 'Slabbing'. At the side of the playground, there was an old stone slab where the older boys grabbed the new boys on their first day, put them on the slab and beat their behinds with their gym shoes. Very brutal. As I walked through the playground gates, feeling very vulnerable, I saw that some of the other boys had already been slabbed because they were crying, I made up my mind I would not cry. I was alone and didn't have our Mavis to fight my battles. Suddenly it seemed it was my turn to be slabbed. The fourth form perpetrators were Brian Greenwood, Joe Hagan and Bobby Henthorne (Dennis' older brother) and some others, they turned and looked at me. I was the smallest of all the children in the school apart from one Bobby Jelly (his real name) who was even smaller than me. They must have taken pity on me for some reason as, mercifully, they left me alone and I was never slabbed. (That didn't stop me from slabbing other kids when I reached the fourth year).

After that first day at Crompton House, life at the big school wasn't so bad. Our Mavis was always there to rely on, and as Dennis and Glenys Henthorne started the same day as me, I had my friends. I made friends quite easily and before long I had quite a few. There was John Bodkin, who I still see from time to time, (the local butcher in Shaw); Dennis Howarth, who I met up with after about twenty years and he looked just the same as he did when he was seventeen, Lucky bloke! There are so many others I could mention, but if I did, there'd not be enough space for me!

One particular day when I was still in my first year at Crompton House, we had just left at four o'clock and were making our way home. Down the back of the school was a dirt track which was the short cut. This was where fights were had and this day it was my turn. I was fighting with another boy and was getting the better of him when a voice boomed out from the top of the lane, "Harper!" We immediately stopped fighting, and some ran off, but we stood there and looked up to see Mr. Stanhope, a young teacher who all the girls were infatuated with.

'Harper, see me in the morning at the first lesson,' he shouted.

That night I didn't sleep. Inside I was panicking. It was the first time I had been in trouble at the school. I kept wondering what was going to happen.

In the morning we caught the 'little F' bus to go to school, I felt tortured, I hadn't told our Mavis, so she didn't have a clue what I was going through. We arrived and went in for Assembly and all through the morning prayers I kept sneaking looks at Mr. Stanhope who didn't look at me once. After that we all filed out of the hall and made our way to class, my first class was Religious Studies with who else but Mr. Stanhope! I sat through the whole class wondering when he was going to call me out and cane me in front of everyone, it was the longest time, and he didn't even mention my name, he just kept looking at me. At the end of the lesson he dismissed us all and we all stood up to leave, I felt so relieved, I had got away with it. Suddenly he snapped 'Harper!' My mouth went dry and my heart thumped. Now was the time. I slowly turned and looked at him. He stared back at me, then winked,

'Forget about it Harper,' he said, 'And don't let me catch you fighting again.'

'No sir!' I replied and was out of that classroom as fast as an Olympic sprinter.

I had never felt so much relief in my whole life. I couldn't understand why he had let me off. From then on he gained my respect and became one of my favorite teachers. He didn't treat us like children, but more like friends. I realized as I got older that he didn't punish me that day as he knew how much I had put myself through from the fear of being punished. He was a good teacher. And if you do read this, Mr. Stanhope, I want to thank you for your compassion.

During all this time I had continued performing and by now our Mavis had joined me and we had become a duo, originally named, 'Bobby and Mavis'. We became quite successful for a twelve and fourteen year old boy and girl. My parents had obtained a license from the education authority which allowed us time out of school to entertain and we traveled all over the place, mostly at the weekend as a professional act. We would even go over to Yorkshire to work in the clubs. My mother would chaperone myself and our Mavis and we'd set off and catch the train to Sheffield, and from there we would go over to the club and perform. After we had finished our performance we would be paid and that would pay for our digs for the night, we would play a different club the following night and the money from that gig would pay our train fare home with a little spending money left over.

One weekend we were booked to perform at the same club for the duration, with a Sunday lunch-time performance also thrown in, which meant extra money. As usual we caught the train to Sheffield and when we arrived at the club, which was quite busy, we went on stage and stormed them. When we had finished my mother asked the Concert Secretary for our money, but he told her that we wouldn't be paid until we had completed the weekend. I can still see my poor mothers' face. Panic and defeat swept across it at the same time. We had no money to get back home and we had no money to pay for digs for the night. We sat in the dressing room and then my mother stood our Mavis and me in front of her and explained the situation. To me as a child this was a great adventure, but to my mother it must have been a problem which seemed insurmountable. There she was, penniless, with two children, somewhere in Sheffield looking at the prospect of spending the night on the street. It was ironic, really, there was our Mavis with me on stage with the audience going wild and my poor mother sitting backstage worrying and wondering what on earth we were going to do. She told the Concert Secretary of our predicament but he told her he couldn't help because it was against the clubs' policy, (nice man, eh?) Everything must have seemed hopeless to my mother. At the end of the night we had no option but to stand at the entrance to the club and tell people we had no money and ask if someone could possibly put us up for the night. How degrading for my mother, she must have felt like a beggar. Anyway God was smiling on us because a kind couple said they could take my mother and Mavis, but they had no room for me. Thankfully God smiled once more when the organist from the club said he would take me in. Our problem was solved and we said our goodbyes. I knew that my mother was extremely worried because she had never been separated from her children before, but, as I said before, it was a great adventure for me. We arranged to meet the following day at the club and waved to each other as they went off in their direction and I went in mine. We reached the organists house and his wife made such a fuss of me that I felt like a king. She made me cocoa and gave me cakes, it was terrific. Praise God I was safe there and look back fondly on the memory.

Sunday morning arrived too quickly and we set off for the club. When we arrived my mother was waiting anxiously. She welcomed me with open arms and then attacked me with a barrage of questions.

Was I alright?

Had I been a good boy?

Had I given any cheek?

Before I had time to answer, the organist put his arm around my shoulder and told my mother she should be very proud of me, as I had been a very good boy.

We finished the lunchtime show and had to find some way to spend the afternoon until it was time for the evening performance. So, with no money to go anywhere or do anything, we spent the afternoon in Sheffield bus station and watched the buses going to and from there various destinations, how riveting! When the evening came we went back to the club and we went down very well with the audience. The Concert Secretary paid my mother and for the first time that weekend we were independent. I believe I learnt a lesson that weekend and from then on strove to be independent of other people, to ask no man for anything and to be my own man. It wasn't until later that I realized being dependant on someone could be a good thing.

By the time I was thirteen our career had really begun to take off. A cousin of mine by the name of Wally Harper who had been a circus clown but now was a professional comedian had taken us under his wing and started to manage us. We were doing warm-ups for BBC radio, which meant we were able to meet all the great stars of the day such as Ronnie Hilton, Lita Rosa, Jimmy Clitheroe and countless others. A television producer by the name of Billy Scott Comber had also shown much interest in us and began teaching us a comedy routine based around the song 'I'm forever blowing bubbles' which meant our Mavis singing it straight with me doing the comedy. We had to go down to the BBC each weekend to rehearse the routine and Mr. Comber told us that when we were ready he would put us on a popular television show named, Comedy Bandbox. It looked as though I had a very promising career ahead of me. All that year I did the warm ups, practiced the comedy routine and worked the clubs as well as going to school as often as I could.

It was around this time when we received a booking for the Isle of Man. We were booked to appear as the resident act in the Majestic Hotel for a whole fortnight. Since everything was paid for, the whole family decided to make it a holiday. The Majestic Hotel was a magnificent place overlooking the harbour, we lived like kings for the entire fortnight, and it was a real treat. At the same time, they had a big talent competition running and the prize was a recording contract and an audition for a television show. As we were the resident act at the hotel and classed as professionals, we were not allowed to enter. The talent competition was for amateurs only. One day a good-looking young man arrived at the hotel on an old Lambretta scooter with a beautiful girl on the back. He asked the manager if he could enter the talent competition, but was told that he was too late; it was on that night. He looked very sad and my father felt so sorry for him, so he stopped him from leaving and promised to put in a word for him with the manager. The young man waited while my father went and tried to persuade the manager to let him enter. After a while my father came back and told the young man that he was in the competition. He was delighted and went on to win the lucrative prize. His name was Gerry Dorsey, who later changed his name to Englebert Humperdink. Many years later Englebert gave a guest appearance on one of our television shows and I reminded him of the competition in the Isle of Man, he remembered and thanked me for it.

My life was soon to change. I reached fourteen and suddenly began to notice girls. More importantly to me

55

then was the discovery of Rock and Roll. Instantly Little Richard, Chuck Berry and Jerry Lee Lewis became my heroes. All theses stars made a big impression on me. James Dean and Elvis were mean and moody and that's what I wanted to be. I started to think that anybody in show-business was a sissy. To me Elvis and James Dean were 'real', I couldn't imagine them in show-business, doing what I was doing, so it was time for me to 'grow up' and get moody. The first thing I had to do was to tell our Mavis that I didn't want to do the act anymore.

I told her that I couldn't be bothered with all that any more and she accepted it without any protest. Little did I realize that she had discovered boys and Rock and Roll for herself.

The first thing I did was to get a jar of Brylcreem and plaster it on my head. The idea was to get the rock and roll hairstyle. You had to comb your hair up at the sides and down over the middle of the forehead to create an 'elephants' trunk' at the back we styled it into a DA, combing each side back to make a parting down the centre of the back of the head. The Brylcreem was used so thickly that your hair was so greasy it didn't move when put into place.

This all worked fine on guys with straight hair, but mine was curly and the Brycreem made it even curlier. So you can only imagine how I must have looked. I looked as though I'd had a fright. Nevertheless I didn't see it this way and I felt good.

The next part of my 'Rock and Roll' uniform to arrive was my drainpipe trousers. You couldn't get trousers tighter than these. And I have to tell you, I don't have the greatest legs in the world. Then were the shoes which were named 'brothel-creepers', my bootlace tie and, the final touch, no rock 'n' roller would be seen dead without his shirt collar turned up. Now I was really mean and moody.

Crompton House School sadly would not accept this

form of dress and there we still had to be dressed as schoolchildren.

There was one girl at school I was really attracted to. I had a secret crush on her. She was gorgeous with long blonde hair. The only thing was that she came from the posh part of town and I came from the opposite end. She seemed out of my reach. Every day I would see her running down the corridors and my heart would melt. Of course I didn't tell anybody except for Dennis Henthorn. I didn't want anyone to think I wasn't cool, or mean and moody. So, knowing she could never be mine, I just kept my distance and admired her from afar.

One day Dennis came over to me in class and asked if I wanted to go to the cinema that night. He was taking a girl out and asked if I would go with them. I told him no. No way was I going to be the gooseberry. He told me not to worry; he'd got me a date as well. I was a bit worried, what had he done? Then he told me who he'd got me the date with, it was her, the girl of my dreams! He told me he'd asked her if she would go out with me and she said yes! My heart started thumping, I had never felt so excited in my life. That evening, I spent hours getting ready, I styled my best ever elephants trunk and my drainpipes were perfectly pressed. Eventually I was ready. I wore a new casual jacket I had just bought, it was brilliant, because when I turned my collar up it came halfway up my face. The only problem was that it was made from plastic, so I could smell plastic all the time. But that didn't matter, it was a true rock 'n' roll jacket. (When I think about it, I must have looked a right little Wally. I was only about four foot eight.)

I met them all at the Princess Cinema (Prinnie) and when I saw her I couldn't speak, she looked beautiful. I just nodded my head in her direction and looked the other way. That must have made me seem really mysterious. We all went into the cinema and sat in the back row, Dennis with his date and me with mine. The lights went down and the movie started. I hadn't even plucked up the courage to speak to this girl yet. My mind was ticking over at a hundred miles an hour. Should I hold her hand? Should I ask her if she wanted an ice cream? No! I thought I'm going for the big one; I'm going to put my arm around her. After about ten minutes of courage building I slowly sneaked my arm around the back of the seats and onto her shoulders. To my amazement she didn't resist. There I was, me, sitting with my arms around my dream girl. My confidence was now at an all time high, so I decided I would go for the really big one, the kiss!

I waited until the time was right, and slowly turned my head towards her. She looked back at me and I knew that this was it, now was the time. We slowly leaned towards one another, lips puckered, I didn't want to miss a moment, and so as she closed her eyes, I kept mine open. Then at the crucial moment, we kissed, or did we? Her eyes shot open. My collar had come between us. Her lips were kissing one side of the collar and mine the other. I can still see her eyes looking at me over the collar. I'm sure she must have felt nauseated by the smell of plastic. My confidence was now in tatters, the image of the mean and moody boy was now gone, I was now the boy who smelled of plastic. Too much for me, with all my credibility gone, I ran out of the cinema. Even my elephants' trunk was fading. I had just blown my chances with my dream girl and I hadn't even spoken to her.

The next day Dennis asked me what had happened. There was no way I could tell him the truth, so I said I didn't like her, that I fancied someone else instead. I wished that I had told the girl in the first place that I liked her instead of trying to be something I wasn't. But life's like that and I wasn't the first person to pretend to be something I was not.

1959 was one of my favourite years. At fifteen years

old I was in my final year at school. The careers officer had been around and had given me up as hopeless. I decided he didn't know what he was talking about; he didn't know rock and roll. Unknown to my mother who would have killed me, I became a bit of a rebel at school, like most teenagers I didn't care much about the future, only the present.

One Monday morning we had to assemble in Mr. Davis's class. I didn't like Mr. Davis, he was my least favourite teacher. A big man, he could frighten people with just a look and this morning he was scowling more than ever. When the class was seated, he told them that on the previous Friday they had all misbehaved and as a punishment had to do a half hour detention after school. Well, I thought this was extremely unfair to me as I hadn't been in school that day. I decided to tell him and put my arm up to get his attention, he ignored me.

"Excuse me sir!" I shouted.

He looked at me with venom in his eyes. I was sure he hated me more than anyone in the class.

"What is it, Harper?" He snapped.

"Well, sir" I began, "I wasn't at school last Friday, so I don't think its right that I should have to do detention."

He just glared at me. "You will do detention with all the rest of them, Harper." He said.

Now all my life I have believed in people being fair and doing the right thing, I thought that he was being unfair and decided to tell him.

"But sir" I shouted from the back, "I wasn't there that day, so I won't be stopping for detention."

The whole class fell silent; at last somebody had stood up to this bullying teacher. Mr. Davis looked up sharply from the book he was marking, he looked as though he was about to kill me. But I wasn't going to back down, I was right.

"Harper!" he screamed, "Come here".

It was the longest walk from the back of the classroom

to the front and everyone was looking at me. I was beginning to wonder whether I should have kept my big mouth shut and done the detention instead. It was too late now and I knew I was right. He was still glaring when I reached his desk.

"You, boy, will do as you are told and will stay in for detention with the others after school."

"No I won't sir!" I replied defiantly.

"Yes you will!" Mr. Davis bellowed.

"Oh, ___," I said, swearing at him in my meanest voice, a swear word that ends in off.

The rage seemed to rise from his toes as he stood to his full height of about six-foot.

"What did you say?" He screamed.

"Nothing sir" I replied innocently, I turned to the class, "Did I?"

And to my relief they all replied in one voice, 'No sir'.

This was all too much for Mr. Davis, already it looked as though his face was about to burst under the pressure. He reached out and tried to grab me, but I dodged his grasp, I knew by now that I had gone too far and it was time for a quick exit. I bolted out of the classroom, thinking I was safe, but when I turned around there was Mr. Davis in hot pursuit. Suddenly there was this demented giant of a man chasing me through the corridors of the school. I had never ran as fast before, but he was catching up, so I headed up the stairs to the headmasters office. When I reached there I didn't even knock, but just barged in with Mr. Davis right behind me.

Mr. Hargreaves, the Headmaster, must have wondered what on earth was happening. It must have seemed that a hurricane had entered his office. There we stood, me, a small boy, followed by this giant of a man, both gasping for breath. It seemed to take Mr. Hargreaves a couple of minutes to find his voice, before he finally asked what on earth was going on.

Mr. Davis jumped right in first, he told Mr. Hargreaves

that I had refused detention and I had sworn at him in front of the whole class. I had always thought Mr. Hargreaves a fair man and hoped that today would be no exception. He asked me if what Mr. Davies had said was true and what had I got to say for myself. I stood up straight and put on my most innocent voice, informing him that as I hadn't been in school the day that the class had misbehaved, I didn't feel it was fair for me to be punished. Mr. Hargreaves nodded and said that he understood, but what about the swearing?

This was too tricky to explain my way out of so I lied. I looked straight at the Head-teacher and told him that Mr. Davies was lying and he could go and ask the class if he wanted to.

Mr. Davies exploded, I thought he was going to have a heart attack he was so angry. He ranted that I was disruptive and went on and on exaggerating my behaviour. Mr. Hargreaves finally calmed him down, and told me that this time I had got away with it, he was of the same mind that I shouldn't be punished for something I hadn't done, but, on the other hand he wasn't convinced about the swearing and he believed that I had done this. He explained that we must let the whole matter drop but I must not brag to the other children or then I would be in trouble. He dismissed me and told me to go back to class while he spoke to Mr. Davis.

I left the office feeling as though I had won a major battle. When I got back to the classroom all the other children were waiting to see what had happened. I gave them a broad smile and put my thumbs up, they all cheered. Of course I quickly forgot about the warning Mr. Hargreaves had given me and told them all the details. I became a hero for the day. As for Mr. Davies, I told know what had been said to him by Mr. Hargreaves, but he never looked at me again, and left me alone for the remainder of my time at school, which was fine with me.

At weekends I and a few friends had started to travel up to Oldham, which was around six miles from Shaw. This was big time as Oldham was a town and we came from a village. We went to a place called The Green, which was only a common, but this one had a fairground. The main ride was the Waltzer, and the teddy boys would gather there and listen to the rock and roll music. We were no exception. We'd stand around the Waltzer, pretending to be tough by puffing on one of the five woodbine cigarettes we had just bought around the corner. It was the Green which led me to meet Joan Lynn.

One weekend I spotted a girl I fancied and decided to have a go at pulling her, (that's Teddy boy talk), so I eventually got talking to her and found out that her name was Helen Lavity. We got on very well and she gave me her address. We arranged to meet the following weekend on a date. I thought that this was the beginning of a big romance. When the time came the next weekend, she didn't turn up, I was devastated at being stood up and decided to go and look for her (I was terribly clingy). Dennis Henthorne came with me, we always went around in two's, and searched the streets of Oldham looking for her. When we found the street where she lived I saw a pretty red-haired girl who was on her way to the shops, I asked her if she knew where Helen Lavity lived. She told me that, yes, she knew her and asked why I wanted to know. I explained that I had a date with her, but she had obviously forgotten about it. This girl told me straight that she understood very well what had happened as Helen Lavity was already going out with someone else. I wouldn't go so far as to say that I was heartbroken, but I will admit that my ego took a fair battering and I felt somewhat deflated. I chatted for a while with this girl, with Dennis standing around like a spare part and then we said our farewells.

The following weekend a few mates and I went up to

the Green again and a gang of girls were there. Among them was none other than Helen Lavity and the red-haired girl. It was funny but I found myself looking at the red-haired girl. Eventually the gang of girls split up leaving the red-head and a friend on their own. I put on my best Elvis face and walked over to her and started talking. I felt very much at ease with her, it was as though I had known her for much longer than our two brief meetings. She told me that her name was Joan Lynn and that she didn't have a boyfriend. This was the start of a long courtship which eventually ended when she became my wife.

Our romance was a very hit and miss affair at the beginning. I saw her only at weekends. Funnily enough I had started to see another girl at the same time, one who lived near me in the next village, so this girl I would see during the week, after school and Joan at the weekend. At fifteen, I had no concept of commitment to either one of them. The other girl was called Margaret Fielding and she was very tall. The truth is I had to stand on two bricks just to kiss her. No wonder my arms are longer than they should be, I was carrying those bricks around with me all the time.

One day at school, I hatched a plan to escape. It was sports day and a few of my mates and I, were not very interested in athletics so I knew it would be a very boring day. When the whole school assembled on the playing field, those who were competing were to go into the middle and those who were not were to sit on the perimeter and cheer on the competitors. Now I couldn't see the sense in sitting there cheering for something that I wasn't vaguely interested in. So I told my friends that when we got to the sports field we should all sit at the back. When the sports and cheering began, we should then be able to sneak out under the fence on by one, and hopefully, no-one would notice during all the commotion. I was hoping we would be able to get out and spend the day with Margaret and her friends. My mates readily agreed, so the plan was on.

The moment arrived and we all went down to the sports field and we made certain we sat behind everybody else so we wouldn't be seen. The plan went like clockwork and the cheering started. We all sneaked out and before long we were all on our bikes pedaling towards an afternoon of fun. We spent the day hanging around the bus stop in the centre of the village flirting with the girls, without a thought for the others at the sports day. We thought we were being so clever. Little did we realize...

The next morning came and we went to the school assembly. Mr. Hargreaves was congratulating all the competitors from the day before, explaining to them how he thought they were all very clever. 'Not as clever as us' I thought, smugly, 'we had the afternoon off.' When he had finished his speech, he became very serious, then scanning the room he said, 'Five boys were seen running away from the sports field.'

I began to sweat, I didn't for one moment think we had been seen.

'And now,' he continued, 'would they please make their way to the front of the hall, and take their punishment like the men they think they are.'

I sneaked a look around the room at the others to see what they would do. They were obviously just as frightened because each one was sneaking looks back at me. I decided to take the whole matter into my own hands. I figured that if I started to walk, the others would follow. I took a deep breath and pushed my way through the other children and started the long walk down the centre aisle towards Mr. Hargreaves. A deathly silence fell upon the whole room and I began to feel that I was alone. I quickly turned around and looked to see who was following; no-one at all. I felt totally naked. Even the girls were looking at me as though I were some kind of gremlin. It was too late to turn back now. With every step feeling heavier, I continued on my way to the front, fearful of what Mr. Hargreaves was about to do. Mr. Hargreaves was standing on a stage at the front of the assembly hall. This was where he would address the school and I had to go up on to the stage. I'm sure that by this time I was walking in the same way as I had when I had fallen in the tar. I made my way up the steps and stood in front of him. He looked down at me, but didn't say anything for what seemed like half an hour, but in reality was only a few moments. This just made things worse and I became quite nervous.

'What have you got to say for yourself?' he finally barked,

'Nothing sir' I replied sheepishly, with my head down

'Who were the other boys that were with you?' He was now tapping his cane against his leg, a sure torture tactic in my eyes. I glanced over the room to the others, who were silently pleading with me with their eyes not to tell and looking back at his cane, I didn't answer and awaited the onslaught.

'Harper!' He bellowed his voice amplified by the size of the room, 'I am waiting for an answer.'

Again I refused to say anything.

'Who were the boys who were with you?' he asked once again.

'I was on my own sir' I lied. I didn't dare look at him. This infuriated him more,

'Well, Harper,' he said, directing his voice outward, 'seeing that you say that you were on your own, and I know that you were not, you won't mind taking the punishment for those who were with you then, will you?'

'No sir,' I quivered, dreading what was to come. I closed my eyes, imagining him getting into position, and awaited the command to put out my hand.

'But, Harper, as you were honest enough to come up

here,' I opened my eyes and held my breath, 'I am not going to punish you.'

A flood of relief washed through my body. I had got away with it. I was just processing what he had just said when he carried on,

"But, there were another four boys with you," he said, "You can have their punishment instead." My relief crashed to the ground. My only hope now lay in my mates and I looked up, expecting them to come running forward to own up. I expected too much. I could hear Mr. Hargreaves' voice droning on in the distance, but I was now lost in my own thoughts.

"Harper!" His voice shocked me back to reality. "Did you hear me?" I felt faint,

"No sir."

"I asked you what are four three's."

"Twelve, sir." I answered, now realizing that I was about to get twelve whacks of the cane.

"Very good, Harper, step forward."

I stepped forward and held out my hands. Whack! The cane landed twelve times, six on each hand. I felt as if I had stuck my hands into a bramble bush. I bit my tongue, there was no way I would show that it was hurting me.

When he had finished, I felt as though my hands were on fire. I wanted to cry, but I held my tears back and stood there defiantly. He told me to go back to my place and never to let this happen again. I walked back to my place in the assembly and glanced over at my friends who couldn't look at me. Later on when we were in the playground they apologized and remarked how brave I was to take twelve lashings of the cane. I forgave them, knowing that if I hadn't been so stupid as to walk forward I would have done the same as they had.

Meanwhile my love life took a new twist. Margaret Fielding soon found out that I was also seeing a girl from Oldham and so she finished with me, which resulted in Joan and I becoming much closer and were courting quite seriously. My schooldays were nearly over and I would soon be waving goodbye to Crompton House without many regrets. I had little idea what I would be doing with the rest of my life, but if anybody had tried to tell me then that I would end up as a famous comedian one day, I would have thought *they* were being funny.

Chapter 3

Clock-on Tommy

By the end of 1959 I had left school. As I had no qualifications, I began work in the cotton mill. As it is for most people, it was a strange experience leaving school and going out into the real world. My mother would pack up my sandwiches we would set off to work together. It was the same cotton mill where she worked. The first day I was placed in the cellar where they kept all the bales of cotton. My job was to follow the foreman around and doing any jobs that he asked me to do. At this time I became friendly with a boy who would become my best friend for a long time, Trevor Kershaw. We are still good friends and have been through so much together, I'm thankful that he has been around for me whenever I needed him, and hope he would say the same for me. My sanity would not allow me to remain in that job for too long and shortly afterward I moved on to another cotton mill. This is what I did for the next twelve months, jumping from cotton mill to cotton mill. It didn't really matter to me as by now all I lived for was my social life. I used to meet Joan on Fridays, Saturdays and Sundays and the rest of the time I went out with my friends, we would meet and hang around in Shaw.

One Thursday evening, my mates and I decided to go

into Oldham to see a film. While in the cinema I met a girl and we talked. I could never leave it like that and asked her if she would like to meet me in Shaw the following night. She agreed, so I arranged to meet her at seven o'clock at a place called Wren's Nest in Shaw. Friday came and I suddenly realized I had got two things wrong, first I was supposed to see Joan that night and secondly I had no money to get to Oldham where Joan was. I asked my mother if she could lend me some money, but she didn't have any, so I devised a different plan, one that was sure to get me my bus fare to see Joan.

Seven o'clock arrived and my mates and I were waiting for the bus to arrive at Wren's Nest. As we were waiting I began to worry in case the girl wouldn't turn up, if she didn't my ingenious plan would fail. My worries were unfounded because when the bus arrived, she was on it. I greeted her and we started talking while my mates hung around. After about ten minutes I asked her if she would excuse me for a moment while I spoke with them. I gathered them together and asked if any of them would like to buy my date from me for a shilling, (the price of my bus fare to Oldham and back). A lad by the name of Graham Lees, who we nicknamed Leo, said he would, and gave me a shilling. I explained to the girl I had to go somewhere and that Leo would look after her, but she mustn't worry, I'd be back later!

She was obviously put out by this, and I didn't give her time to argue because I jumped on the bus and was away. (I know what you're thinking, and you're right it was pure selfishness that made me a white slave trader at fifteen.) Anyway after I had seen Joan and caught the bus back to Shaw, I came to my senses and realized just what I'd done. My conscience went into overdrive and I knew what I had done was very wrong and extremely foolish. I began to worry about the girl, so when I reached Wren's Nest I went looking for them. I searched around and went to a wooded area called Dunwood

Park. I couldn't see them, but they were there all right because I could hear them all shouting. I don't know what was happening, and the lads could have been just messing around, but, taking no chances, I knew that I had to get that girl away from them and I wasn't sure how to do it. I had an idea,

"Police" I shouted at the top of my voice. All the lads scattered in different directions, leaving the girl alone. She was fine, but very scared and extremely glad to see me. So much so that she forgot about me selling her for a shilling and allowed me to walk her home. I didn't ever see her again, but for some reason I've never forgotten her.

My courtship with Joan grew more serious as the months went by and I started to see her on a more regular basis. There was only one problem, my friend Trevor didn't have a girlfriend, so more often than not, he used to hold the candle, (play the gooseberry) for Joan and me. One day, Trev and I were talking and he confessed that he had always fancied our Mavis! The next day, I told our Mavis that Trevor fancied her and asked her if she would go out with him. She agreed, but told me she was only doing it to help me out as she didn't fancy him. They've now been married for about forty years. We started to go out as a foursome and became quite inseparable.

This nearly ended one year when me and Trevor decided to go on holiday with his brother and a friend. We had booked to stay at the Golden Sands Holiday Camp in Rhyl. Our accommodation was a beat up old caravan, but this didn't matter at all to me, I was young and had never been away without my parents. So to me this was a real adventure. Our Mavis and Joan saw us off at the bus station and Trev and I acted as if we didn't really want to go, but inside we were very excited. We arrived and settled into the caravan. There were four teenage boys in it so you can imagine what state it was soon in. That didn't matter, we were on holiday without the girls. Yippee!

About a week into the holiday I entered into the talent competition they were running at the camp and won it. The prize was two book-ends, which, by the way, my mother kept for over thirty years. In this competition was a young lady called Moira, whom I found very attractive. True to the old saying, 'When the cat's away, the mice will play,' I began to flirt with her. I was a little disappointed to hear that she was staying with her parents in a caravan not far from ours. I had hoped that she was on her own like me. She then proceeded to tell me that if I went late at night, she would leave her bedroom window open and if I kept very quiet, I could sneak in, her parents would be asleep. Now all this to me was very exciting, not only was I going to get the girl, I was about to become James Bond for the night. The morning of the designated tryst, Trevor awoke feeling very ill. As the day went on he became decidedly worse, so we took him to see the Doctor. The Doctor told him he had caught a virus and gave him some tablets. I tried to look after Trevor with as much compassion as I could muster, but couldn't help thinking about sneaking into Moira's caravan that night. By ten o'clock Trevor was sound asleep, the tablets had caused him to feel drowsy. This was turning out to be some great holiday! In those days you never ever went anywhere without your mates, even on a date, and tonight was no exception. Trevor was coming whether he liked it or not, even if I had to carry him there. I fed him cups of coffee all night, trying to keep him awake. By one thirty in the morning I looked at him and he was fast asleep, I shook him and told him it was time to go. He didn't have any idea where he was going, or what was happening, but followed me out of loyalty. He wasn't much company, he was like zombie. I slowly made my way around the maze of caravans with Trevor following me about like one of the living dead. Eventually we reached Moira's caravan. It was quite eerie in the darkness and so silent, I wondered if this was what a thief felt like.

Gingerly I tapped on Moira's bedroom window and waited for her to open up. There was no reply so I knocked again. Still no window opened up for me. I began to realize that she must have fallen asleep, well, that wouldn't put me off so I knocked once again, only louder this time. Suddenly all the lights in the surrounding caravans lit up, including Moira's. I was out of there as though I was on fire. The last I saw of poor Trevor, he was half asleep wandering towards the swimming pool.

The holiday was soon over and we arrived home. I told Joan that I missed her so much and the next year we would go on holiday together. Then, after we had been back for around a fortnight, Moira came to the village, looking for me. Luckily for me I was in Oldham with Joan, but apparently Trevor had seen Moira in Shaw looking for me and for some reason he took her to our house. My mother asked her who she was and invited her to stay and wait for me, but our Mavis told her in no uncertain terms that I was courting and that was the end of that. Moira left and when I got home I was interrogated. My mother wanted to know who she was, how we met and every detail and our Mavis calling me a two-timer and all the other words which meant the same, with Trevor standing behind the pair of them laughing at me. Everything was smoothed over in the end and Joan didn't ever find out. Perhaps if she had my life would have turned out completely different.

My teenage years found me drifting from job to job, until eventually I started work in the building trade for a chap named John Pogson, (Poggy, to all who knew him). He was a wonderful Christian man who took me under his wing and treated me like a son. He passed away a very long time ago, but to me he was one of the nicest men I have ever had the honour of knowing. I worked for John for around twelve months and then the wanderlust got the better of me again and I moved on. I found a job in an engineering works as a labourer and the money was good so I decided to stay a while.

During this time, my social life took a further twist. Our foursome of Joan and me, Mavis and Trevor had become so close that we decided to form an act. Trevor played the drums while the girls and I did the singing. We had a great time going around the clubs. Our name was 'The Black and Tans, because I was the only one with black hair and Mavis, Trevor and Joan all had flaming red hair. We thought it was a great name, until we worked at an Irish club. I can tell you we didn't go down very well at all, but to tell you the truth we weren't half bad.

My father by this time had lost the majority of his hearing, and though it was an irritation for him, we used this to our advantage and played our records as loud as we wanted. In the lounge we had our record player, an old Dansette, and a beat-up old upright piano. The piano was situated right behind my fathers' chair. I can still recall the nights we would have our favourite Elvis records; 'Jailhouse Rock', and 'A big hunk of love', on at full blast, and we would bop the night away, behind our Dad, who would be in front of us reading his paper, not realizing what was going on at the back of his chair. It all came to an abrupt end when my father announced he was going to try out a hearing-aid, he called it a 'deaf-aid'. We didn't think it would change our lives too much, Mavis and I, but how wrong we were. He went for some tests and they finally agreed to let him have one. He came home with this big piece of plastic protruding from behind his ear, looking ever so proud. We were fascinated by it and began to ask him questions in whispers being as quiet as we could and to our astonishment he answered them. It was wonderful for him to be able to hear again, he said he could now hear the birds singing, something we were so used to and took for granted. We were happy for him and got used to his hearing-aid, even though it was a pity we couldn't play our records full blast anymore. It did have its down side though, one day in the barest of whispers, I asked my mother if she could lend me a pound. Suddenly my fathers' voice boomed out from the lounge,

"No you can't! You've had your spending money." I knew then that I no longer would I be able to get away with anything because my father could hear the smallest whisper in the kitchen, from his chair in the lounge.

By the time I reached the landmark age of eighteen. Our Mavis was already married to Trevor, so that left just me at home. Next door to us lived an old widow by the name of Mrs. Tarkenter and her niece Emmy. She was a lovely old lady, who had always kept herself to herself, but as she got older, she began to lose her mind and go a little crazy. I would every evening arrive home about eleven o'clock after being out with Joan and it began to happen that every evening Mrs. Tarkenter would wait for me. She would stand at her bedroom window, in her long white nightdress, with her wispy, graying black hair flowing around her shoulders and she would beckon to me. It was terrifying. When I was young, I had watched the play, 'Jayne Eyre' on television and the mad woman in the attic had frightened me very much, and this was too spooky for me. Anyway the more Mrs. Tarkenter lost her mind, the bolder she got. One night I arrived home at my usual time and there she was beckoning to me from her window. I ran past her house and down our path as fast as I could to the front door. The worst part was getting my key out and letting myself in, in the darkness. My imagination would always run wild, 'what if she came now? Was she behind me on the garden path? Did she have a knife? I whipped myself into such a panic each night with these thoughts as I fumbled with my key, and this night was no exception. I got in and slammed the door behind me, breathing a huge sigh of relief, tonight I had felt more scared than ever, but at least now I was safe. My mother and father were asleep in bed as usual so, heart still thumping; I made myself a cup of tea and turned on the TV, trying to put her out of my mind. I settled down to watch my favourite program, 'The Twilight Zone'. Just as I was getting into it there came a tapping on the window. It was Mrs. Tarkenter. My heart nearly stopped. It was the first time she had ever done anything like this. My skin began to crawl. I was so terrified I couldn't move. I could hear her moving around outside, trying to find a way in, trying to find a way to get to me. I knew I had to go up and get my dad. But going upstairs posed a problem, the stairs faced the front door, she would see me through the window. I decided to make a dash for it and get my dad, he would know how to handle the situation. As I opened the door to the hall, I could hear Mrs. Tarkenter scratching at the front door, I pressed my back against the wall, I didn't want to her to see me, and I couldn't look at her so I tried to sneak past the front door and creep up the stairs. It was too late, the letterbox opened and she whispered,

"Robert, let me in", I turned around and looked back at the door. She was peering at me through the letterbox, looking right at me and whispering. That was it for me, I shot up the stairs like a bullet. I shook my father in a panic, telling him that Mrs. Tarkenter was trying to get into the house. He probably thought that I was going mad myself. He pulled on his clothes and went downstairs. I stood at the top with my mother, and watched as my father told her off as though she was a little girl and sent her home. She progressively went worse and began to wander around the gardens at night, she began to attack her niece Emmy, who left when she couldn't take any more. She was so tormented; my mother once found her trying to commit suicide and had to stop her. She eventually died and it was very sad as she wasn't found for two days. I do regret not being able to help her more, she really did need caring for but I was so scared of her I avoided her like the plague.

Aged just twenty, Joan and I decided to get married. It was 1964 and our Mavis and Trevor had just had their first child, Beverley. Our Sylvia, by this time, had three children, Glynn, Gail and a newborn daughter, Jayne. With all this happening, we decided we could no longer carry on with the singing act so it came to a natural end. Throughout this time, I had also been attending night school to learn how to be a welder. I wasn't one to sit around with nothing to do, and every night had to be taken up with something.

We had saved up enough money to put a deposit down on a small terraced house in Oldham, which I decided I would decorate myself. Joan was very patient with me as I began work on the bathroom. I was in what I would like to call, my psychedelic period and painted the walls in an array of vivid blues, reds and greens, which I then covered in clear varnish. Can you imagine what it looked like! I was so proud of it then but I was no interior designer. It was definitely unique and I often wonder what the next owners of that house made of it all.

That same year, 1964, was a turning point for another reason. It was the year I met a man who was to become my closest friend for the rest of my life. He was, and still is, the brother I never had. Tommy. I had gone to work that morning, as usual, and, as usual, I was late. I didn't really care, as my mate, Terry Brierly used to clock me in. So I would turn up at the factory late and sneak in behind the machines and nobody was any the wiser. This particular day, I arrived and there was Tommy, standing by the door waiting for someone to show him what to do as it was his first day. I noticed how lonely he looked so I went over to him, and greeted him with the usual Oldham greeting,

"Alright Cock?" he looked at me and nodded, quite friendly. I carried on past him and sneaked behind the machines and got on with my work, not thinking anymore about it.

Fridays were always special because one, we got paid and two, it was the night all the lads got together and went out on the town. It was, and still seems to be, a ritual in northern towns and we called it, originally, the 'lads' night out.' We would all meet up in the centre of Oldham and travel from pub to pub, then after they closed, we would move on to the Candlelight Club. It was a bit of a dive really and quite rough, but then it had a great atmosphere. Friday nights in Oldham in those days were fantastic. It had just one main street, Yorkshire Street, reaching from the top of the town to the bottom, quite a steep hill of around half a mile. There must have been between fifteen and twenty pubs on that stretch and each one had a live group playing there, many of them later went on to become famous, including The Beatles. This was our Friday Night Out, the lads and me hitting every pub on the way down Yorkshire Street, a very lively place to be on Friday nights. After a while we were bored with going to all the same places, week in and week out, but the problem was none of us owned a car, so we were pretty stuck and couldn't get much further afield.

I liked Tommy and noticed he had a car. One day I approached him and asked him if he would like to come out with us all on Friday, he said he would, so now, we had a car to go out in. We were truly going up in the world. I will always remember that little car of Tommy's. It was a Mini. Not just any ordinary Mini, now that would not have suited Tommy. It had all the trimmings, alloy wheels, two radio aerials and chequered racing tape down the sides. It was a great-looking car. He was always a poser! Friday nights took on a different dimension after Tommy agreed to come with us, now we had the freedom to go wherever we wanted.

One day I was offered a booking to sing at a local working men's club by an old friend, the performer in me could not say no and so this began a new season for me on club circuit. I hadn't realized just how much I'd missed being on stage and was happy to get started again. I began to do the clubs at week-ends on my own, I wasn't bad, but not brilliant either, but was quite happy then. I thought life was good and was totally unaware of how things were going to change for me.

It was 1965 and Joan was now expecting our first child. It's strange that when you are young, you just accept that your wife is pregnant and don't notice the beauty of it; you just get on with life. Joan had a fear of hospitals and made the decision to have a home birth. It was some experience, I can tell you. When the time arrived for her to give birth, she told me to go and phone the doctor. She was having labour pains and knew it was the time. I, on the other hand, knew something was happening as *I* was beginning to feel sick and sweaty and suffered a terrible backache. I rushed up the street to the telephone box and called the doctor. He told me not to panic as he would send the midwife around immediately. The midwife arrived soon after and examined Joan, she explained that she wouldn't be ready for quite some time and that she would come back later. Little did we know that Joan would be in labour for twenty-eight hours. Well, I was in a terrible state. I sat downstairs with Joan's dad and Joan stayed upstairs with her mother. Things were much different then, and husbands did not watch the whole birthing process. Eventually the midwife returned and with her help they delivered our first baby. Downstairs was quiet until I heard the baby cry and then the midwife shouted to say that I could go up and see my child. When I entered the bedroom, I first noticed Joan. She looked completely exhausted, which was understandable after twenty-eight hours of labour. Then I saw our child. Joan had given me a son and he was the most beautiful baby I had ever seen. He had a huge curl on the top of his head and the biggest, bluest eyes you ever saw. We named him Robert, not after me but my father. The in-laws took a look at him and then left. Now there was only Joan, the midwife and myself. The midwife gave me some instructions and told me that on the top of the cooker, downstairs, there was a kidney shaped dish with a rubber tube in it, she asked me to sterilize it.

"No problem," I told her, feeling like a very responsible father.

How wrong I was. I went to sterilize the tube. Before long the midwife turned to Joan and remarked that she could smell something burning. Joan said that she could too. So the midwife came downstairs to check that everything was as it should be and found this responsible father fast asleep on the couch and the rubber tube burning in the dish. I was very young really so being irresponsible came naturally to me for the next few years. The next morning Joan's mother arrived and found me perched on the edge of the bed, in my donkey jacket, with my guitar.

"What the hell do you think you are doing?" my mother-in-law demanded.

I told her. I was serenading my son. (He wasn't even twenty-four hours old and already I wanted him to know how talented his dad was.) Next to arrive was the midwife to see how mother and baby were doing. She asked me if Joan had eaten her breakfast yet. Oh no, I said, I had forgotten. We had nothing in, so I dashed up the road to the corner shop and bought the first things I saw for her to eat that morning, a jam roll cake, a chocolate cake and a slab of angel cake. Pure luxury, I thought. I sliced them all into pieces, set them out on two dinner plates and proceeded to take them upstairs. I felt very proud and was so glad to help. I can still see the faces of my mother-in-law and the midwife when I walked into the room. Their mouths dropped open and they stared at the assortment of cakes. Joan's face didn't flinch as she was already used to me by now.

"Are we having a party?" the midwife eventually asked.

"No," I replied, this had really confused me, "its Joan's breakfast".

The two women looked at me as if I had lost my mind. What they didn't understand was that when I saw Joan looking so exhausted after having the baby, I knew that she'd need the sugar to give her energy, hence the cakes. As you might have guessed, the cakes went uneaten and my mother-in-law went downstairs and made Joan a nice cooked breakfast. I can't remember if she made me one, probably not.

That year I was getting more gigs than usual. It was great. I was out working nearly every weekend. Slowly, show business began to take over my life, so much so, that even when I was at my day job it was all I could think about. It would eventually be the downfall of my marriage. Even though I was working day and night, I still went out with Tommy and the boys each Friday, occasionally I went out in the week too. I was spending less and less time at home with my family.

When I used to do a gig at the weekend, more often than not Tommy would show up with his wife and over a period of time we became close friends. Joan and I would visit Tommy and his wife at their home and vice versa. Up to this point, Tommy was not in show business, but it was obvious to me that he was very keen.

Around the same time I became friendly with a lovely man by the name of

Stan Moores, who worked on one of the saw machines. In his spare time, Stan played the organ around the club circuit. He was a great little jazz pianist, so I asked him if he would write some music for me. He agreed and invited me up to his house to rehearse. When I arrived there, I was surprised to see that he was married to a girl who went to Lilac nursery with me. What a small world!

One day Stan told me he had been offered a resident gig at the small working men's club not far from where I lived. He said it was a good gig because it was for every Friday, Saturday and Sunday. There was only one problem, he explained, he needed a drummer. This sounded very good to me as I was becoming tired of jumping from club to club, wondering if I'd get any more gigs or not, and it would also mean I was closer to home. I told him that I was available. He was surprised and asked me if I could drum, of course I can, I told him. I had learned to drum while I was in the Black and Tans, practicing on Trevor's drums. I omitted to tell him that I'd never played professionally before, but with my ego, that was only a minor problem. It was settled. He told me I could have the gig and that I could start the following Friday. The only problem was that I didn't have a drum-kit. Stan told me not to worry as there was a kit in the club which I could use.

The following Friday soon came and I arrived at the club ready to begin my career as a drummer. Luckily for me, that night the double-act which performed, did all Roy Orbison numbers and I found that quite easy to do. I also sang while playing the drums, between acts and my big number was 'Whiter Shade of Pale' by Procul Harum. The members of this club hadn't seen anyone do this before and so I became quite a success there. I thought I would be able to settle there, but I'm just not made that way.

Each Friday, Tommy and the boys would come into the club to see me, then they would leave around ten-thirty and go up to the Candlelight Club, and I would stay behind to finish the gig. This was fine by me for the first few weeks, and then I began to feel that I was missing out on all the fun. I can still see them now as they all stood up from their seats at ten-thirty, gave me a wave and left, leaving me on the drums backing some old lady singing, 'I want to be Bobby's girl', which got more and more awful as the song went on. I stuck this for about two months and then I told Stan I was leaving. He was a good man and he understood. So there I was back on the road doing the clubs and every Friday up at the Candlelight.

One day Tommy and his wife invited me and Joan up to his house for tea. We accepted, put our Robert in his carrycot and off we went. We ate and then sat around talking and listening to records. During one of the records I noticed Tommy tapping along to it. I mentioned that I could see that he had some rhythm and if he could get hold of a kit of drums, I would teach him how to play. I didn't think any more about it until two days later when he came into wok and said he had borrowed some money from his father-in-law and bought a drum kit; was I prepared to teach him? I must admit that I was taken aback with how keen he was. I told him I would teach him, so I started to go up to his house and within a couple of weeks, had taught him the basics of drumming. We had become quite close friends by now, so I approached Stan Moores and asked him if he would like to start a trio, him on piano, Tommy on drums and me singing. He was very interested and said he would like to give it a go. I told Tommy that we were in a trio and he was the drummer and he was overjoyed, so we all got together and started rehearsing at the local working men's club. We didn't have a name at this point so decided to call ourselves 'The Stan Moores Trio!' And that was the beginning of our working partnership.

If I had known the heartaches it was about to bring me, I might have stayed a drummer in the working men's club up the road. But I was ambitious and worked hard. We rehearsed every Wednesday and slowly we got better and better, but the gigs just didn't seem to come. We occasionally did the odd wedding, but we weren't doing anything to set the world alight. I had done more gigs when I was on my own. The only good thing to come out of it was that I heard Tommy sing. So we decided to change the act so that Tommy would sing a couple of songs with me on the drums and then we'd swap over and I would sing a couple. It seemed to work because a local pub called the Fitton Arms asked us if we would play there every Sunday night. We were only too delighted and stayed there for about two months, improving all the time. Then one day Stan came in and said he had been offered a residency at another club and he felt he had to take it, we told him that we understood and parted the best of friends.

This now left Tommy and me on our own. We decided not to bring in another pianist but we would go out as a singing double act. We gathered as many songs together as we knew and rehearsed them at Tommy's house. After a while we felt as though we were quite good, although when I look back, we were rubbish. We set off on the usual rounds doing auditions anywhere and for anybody. We didn't have a name so we bantered names around and finally I came up with what must be the worst name in the world for a double act. Bobby and Stevie Rhythm! I told you it was bad, but at the time we thought it was a great name.

We were so excited to be a double act that we decided we just had to look like professionals. So off we went to Burton's the tailors and bought two sets of grey slacks and blazers on hire purchase. We took them home and had two badges made, one for each of us. The badges were my 'brainwave' and it turned out all wrong. I had the idea that we should each wear a badge, sewn on to our blazers, mine with BR, for Bobby Rhythm and

Tommy's had SR, Stevie Rhythm. We had this done and felt like a million dollars. That week we had an audition at a club, so we set off with our new set of stage clothes and went up to the bar for a drink. We hadn't even got up to sing yet when a woman came up to Tommy, looked at his badge and said, in the loudest voice you have ever heard,

'Do you work for the SR toothpaste company?'

Poor Tommy didn't know where to look. He was so embarrassed. She then looked at my badge, but before she could say anything I said,

'Before you open your mouth, no, I do not work for British Rail!' I then told her in no uncertain terms that we were a double act, Bobby and Stevie Rhythm. And we were performing there that night.

'Well,' she retorted, 'I hope that you sing better than you are dressed.'

I think that was the first and last time Tommy and I wore those outfits. We also decided a change of name wouldn't do us any harm, so we changed it to the Sherrell Brothers, (after the Sherrells, a popular Tamla Motown group). I agree it wasn't much better, but at least wouldn't get asked if we worked for a toothpaste company or British Rail. We later had another name change and became the 'Harper Brothers'.

We continued to work at the factory as usual, and at weekends went on various auditions and working. Slowly our diary began to fill up as we got more bookings, and eventually we were able to stop auditioning.

At work, as a welder I was still a bit of a rebel, and one day things didn't turn out exactly as I'd planned. We had started work as usual this particular morning and everything seemed quite normal. It was winter and it was quite cold in the factory, and I thought it wasn't fair that we should be working in such cold conditions so I decided to do something about it. (The truth was I felt rather bored and wanted something different to happen.) I approached Terry Brierly and told him I was sure that we shouldn't be working in these cold conditions. He agreed and asked me what we could do about it, so I explained that we should approach the management and tell them that either they put on some heating or we would all walk out. He suggested that I spread the word around the lads and if they were all with us, then that's what we would do. I immediately began to go to everyone finding out who was with us and who wasn't. To my surprise, everyone I spoke to was with us. The only person that I hadn't told was Tommy, so I went to his workbench and told him our plans. He told me that he would do what everyone else was doing. All stations go! Inside I felt a growing excitement as now we could get our own back on the foreman and the manager, Jack Moore, who I believed had never liked me, he could have, but I felt deep inside that he didn't.

When the morning break came, we all crowded into the canteen and began to discuss our plan of operation. It was decided that after our break we should all go back to the factory floor and put down our tools. This was very exciting for me, it was such a drama. After the break we all went into the factory and put down our tools, then stood around talking. It wasn't long before Jack Moore and his team of foremen came down on to the shop floor. He stood on a nearby packing case and we all gathered around him. He then demanded to know what was going on. Everybody looked at me and I in turn looked at Tommy. Remember, Tommy had nothing really to do with all this; he was just going along with everyone else. Tommy, true to form, took control. He spoke up and told Jack Moore that it was too cold to work and unless the management turned on some heating, it had been decided we would all go on strike. Jack Moore glared at us and told us all that what we were doing was wrong and we should work until lunch-time and then discuss the problem. Some of the men sheepishly began to walk back to work, but stopped when Tommy said, we would be prepared to work until lunch-time, but then, if the heating was still off, we would walk out. Jack Moore just laughed and walked off. We all went back to work determined to stick to our guns.

When lunch-time came, we all had our lunch and went back into the factory. As we made our way back into the building, Jack Moore was standing with his foreman watching us. We all clocked on and felt that it was as cold as before. All the lads looked at me again and once again I turned to Tommy. Tommy stepped forward and asked Jack Moore if the heating had been turned on. He said it hadn't and went on to say he had no intention of putting it on and if we didn't like it, we knew what we were to do. This was what I was waiting for. I made my way out to the clocking machine with Tommy and the lads behind me. We clocked out one by one and walked out of the door defiantly. When we got outside we found that there were only six of us. I looked back into the factory and all the other lads had given in and had started work again. Out of one hundred men only six of us had gone on strike. We were Tommy, Terry Brierly, Ronnie Ravey, Eric Mullins, Jack Minton and myself. We all knew in our hearts that this would mean the sack. Well, there was nothing left to do except go to the pub. (Which always seemed to be the answer.) Later that night and a couple of pints heavier I arrived home and told Joan what had happened, hastening to add that all the other men had been cowards and the six of us were the real heroes. She listened patiently and then said that I would have to go and get another job as I now had a family to keep. A couple of days went by and I received a letter. On the envelope was the name of the factory and knew that this was the letter telling me that I had been sacked. Much to my surprise when I opened the letter, they were asking me to go back, along with the other five who had walked out. They also wrote that there would be no repercussions over what had taken place, this was great news we felt that we had won a great victory.

The following morning we went back to the factory, feeling very smug. We had fought the system and won. What fools we were, two days later Tommy was called into the manager's office and fired. He was told that he had been the ringleader of the strike, and that they didn't want any troublemakers at their factory. I felt really guilty because it was me who had started all this trouble, and all that Tommy had done had voiced our opinions. I went straight to the management to tell them it had been me, but they were adamant, Tommy had to go.

Tommy left and before long, every one of the ringleaders, myself included, had gone too. This didn't break up the strong friendship we had, quite the contrary, Tommy, Terry Brierly, Ronnie Ravey and me would always, for some reason find ourselves working together at the same engineering works. Our friendship grew. We continued working the clubs at night and working as welders during the day.

There was only one bad time for me during that period. I was out of work and was having difficulty finding a job, it was nearing Christmas and I needed money to buy Robert some presents. I saw an advert in the paper for coal baggers. I couldn't afford to be choosy so I went for it and got the job. The drawback was that I had to work through the night, that didn't bother me, I was just happy to have any job. The snow was on the ground when I arrived at this old factory. It was a run-down old place with no windows. Obviously, here there was no heating, but there would be no industrial action from me. I needed the money too much.

I walked into the building and couldn't believe my eyes. About twenty men were standing there all ready to start work. I looked at the men and recognized them as some of the villains and hard-cases from around Oldham. I felt a little out of my league, but at least I had a job. The foreman came over and pointed to some huge mounds of coal and told us to pick someone to work with. He then proceeded to tell us that we wouldn't be getting a wage but would be paid according to how much coal we bagged. Some of the men walked out, but not me, this was a lifeline. At least I'd be taking a wage home every week, I thought.

This other man and I got two shovels and went to the biggest mound of coal we could find and began to bag coal as though our lives depended on it. We worked all through the night with no break, bagging one bag of coal after another. By the morning my arms felt as if they had been tied to the Titanic.

Eventually the morning came and the foreman said we could stop work. He told us to gather around him as he had something to say. He proceeded to tell us that we had worked so hard that they had enough bags of coal to last them for three months and we wouldn't be needed any further. He was sacking us. My heart felt as though it was going to drop out of my shoes. There I was; a tradesman with a young child, and no job. I felt that my life couldn't get any worse. But believe me, it did.

The foreman paid us what we had earned that night and we all left. I walked home that morning with three pounds in my pocket, wondering what I was going to tell Joan. I had been ripped off and there was nothing I could do about it.

Someone was surely looking out for me because just a day later, my friend Terry Brierly came to our house and told me he had been offered a job as foreman at an engineering firm. He was gathering the lads back together again, so Tommy, Ronnie Ravey and I started work at this place and it felt good to be back in my trade. By this time Tommy and I had become quite a decent act, and we worked every weekend.

One day while at the factory, my cousin, Wally Harper walked in. He looked at Tommy and me, and told us we were stupid. He wanted to know why we would work in all that smoke and grime when we could make so much more money as professionals. We explained to him that we both had young families, going professional would be too much of a risk. The following weekend was a bank holiday and he told us that he could get us good money for the Friday, Saturday, Sunday and Monday in South Wales, doing the social clubs. We laughed at him, we could get double-time for working the full weekend in the factory, it wouldn't be worth our while. He then told us that all our food and accommodation would be provided as well.

We thought this over and realized that if all that he said was true, we really could get a lot more than working in the factory. So we agreed to do it. We planned our excuses to give to the foreman as to why we would not be in work and got ourselves ready for the big weekend. It would be the first ever time that Tommy and I had been out of Oldham with the act, and the first of many times we were to be away from home.

Tommy and I set off for our adventure to South Wales feeling as though we were entering the twilight zone. In way we were. We arrived at a little village just outside Swansea, and asked Wally to take us to the hotel as we were feeling tired from the journey. I should have known then that something was wrong, because Wally's eyes hit the ground. Tommy was suspicious and asked him if he definitely had got somewhere for us to stay. Wally replied that he had and proceeded to take us up into the mountains. We seemed to be going for hours when suddenly we found ourselves in a field at the top of a mountain. At the other end of the field were two tents. Suddenly out of one of the tents four children came running to greet us, and I recognized them as Wally's children. So that's why we had come here, I thought, to visit Wally's children. We should get to the hotel after this. After we had played with the children for a while

Tommy asked Wally to take us to our hotel now as it was going dark. Then Wally hit is with the bombshell. We didn't have a hotel, he told us, and so the other tent was ours. I couldn't believe my ears. Tommy went on to give Wally an ear bashing but there was nothing we could do about it, as we didn't have any money until we had done the first gig. We agreed, with clenched teeth, that as soon as we had some money we would move into a hotel. Wally tried to make the peace by telling us he would provide the food. He was a loveable rogue and we found it hard to be annoyed with him for long.

Wally left, saying he would go and get the breakfast for the next day and Tommy and I went to look at the tent that we would spend the night in. One look inside and we knew that there was no way we would be sleeping in that, it was filthy and stank so bad that even a wild animal would have refused to shelter in it. Tommy and I decided we would sleep in the car for the night. We settled ourselves in, Tommy in the front and me in the back then talked until the early hours about families and things and drifted off to sleep. Morning came and we awoke to Wally shouting us for breakfast. When we saw what he had for us, we couldn't believe our eyes. He had brought us bananas and morning coffee biscuits for breakfast. (Boy, this was living, and Joan thought I must have been having a great time.) It was absolutely pointless arguing with Wally, so we just accepted the situation and ate our bananas.

The night came and we set off, leaving Wally and the kids, to do our first club in South Wales. It was situated in one of the valleys, miles from anywhere. I hadn't known that Wales had so many mountains. We eventually arrived and told the committee who we were, and they told us that we were have to do three spots, meaning we would have to do three different acts. We agreed and sat in the dressing room, waiting to go on. The time came and we went on. We thought we had done alright, but obviously we were wrong. When we came off stage the committee was waiting for us. They told us. They told us in no uncertain terms that we were rubbish and that we were the worst act they'd ever had at the club. It was the first time that Tommy and I had ever experience anything like this. Back home in Oldham, when we did the clubs, there were always a few of our mates with us, so we always went down well. But this was different, because now we were on our own.

We felt so devastated. The committee gave us a couple of pounds for the spot we had just done and told us to get out. Our pride shattered, we packed our stage suits into our bags and crept out of the club with our tails between our legs. Everybody in the club was glaring at us and we felt as though we had committed murder or something. I don't think Tommy or I spoke a word for the next couple of hours, we were dumbstruck. We had only made a couple of pounds so any thought of a hotel was out, so we got into the car and made a silent journey back to the shabby tents on the top of our mountain. So much for our first performance in South Wales. Tommy, ever the optimist, said it could only get better. He was so wrong, it only went worse.

The next morning, Wally came to us and asked us how we had done, we told him what had happened and he told us that every act has to be paid off (as he called it) to be able to call themselves pro's. I quickly told him that's alright for pro's, but we weren't pro's. That night we set off for the second club in South Wales and the same thing happened. Again we were paid off. This was getting ridiculous. Slowly all the confidence we had began to slip away. The same thing happened at every club we did that weekend except for the Sunday lunch-time show and we managed to last that one out. So out of the five clubs we had come down to do, we got paid off at four of them.

The long weekend was finally over, and Tommy and I

gladly set off for home. On the way back to Oldham we talked about packing it all in. We were going back home with a paltry twelve pounds in our pockets, ten pounds less than we had set out with. We knew deep down in our hearts that we wouldn't give up though, we loved it, even when it was this bad, though it would be a long time before we would return to South Wales, the bruises to our ego's were just too big.

We did go back eventually, and returned many times, but the memory of that weekend will stay, firmly fixed, in our memories forever. South Wales is now a place where we work a lot and is one of our favourite places to perform in Great Britain.

Back at work we lied, telling our mates that we had done really well and the clubs wanted us to go back down and perform at a future date. (If only they'd known the truth).

On the home front everything seemed to be going fine. Robert had grown up into a toddler and had become my little mate. Tommy and I continued working at the factory and doing the pubs and clubs at weekends. When I look back, I realize that Joan wasn't seeing much of me and it would only get worse. Maybe our marriage began to crumble even then, but neither of us realized it. The cracks would soon start to appear over the next few years as I invested more and more time in my dream of becoming a star, while our domestic life came under increasing strain.

Chapter 4

The Professionals

Looking back, the turning point in my career happened one Friday night in a club in Stockport, Cheshire. As usual Tommy and I were having our Friday night out with the boys and we had decided to go to this club. I did not realize that what would happen that night would change my forever.

When we arrived at the club it was packed out. We managed to find a seat in a corner and after getting our drinks we sat back to watch the acts who would be performing there that night. After a couple of pints some of the lads started suggesting that Tommy and I got up on the stage because we were better than the acts who were booked there. We weren't really, but thankfully our mates thought we were. (If they hadn't put us forward, we would have volunteered anyway!) Terry Brierly approached the man in charge and told him that he had two mates with him who wanted to get up and sing. The man in charge was very gracious and told Terry that we could get up after the girl singer who was on next. Terry came back and told us and Tommy and I got very excited. This was not the usual type of place we were used to playing. It was a nightclub and we did pubs and working men's clubs. When the time came we went on stage and proceeded to storm them, left them shouting for more and went back to our seats. We knew that we had done well when the man in charge of the club came over and asked if we would return there as a paid act. We sat there for a while basking in our glory, when a man at the far side of the room beckoned us over. We went, thinking that maybe he was a booker from another club and wanted to book us. How wrong we were! When we reached his table, we could tell that he was more than a club booker. He was wearing a mohair suit and sported gold watch and cufflinks on his shirt. To us this was a wealthy looking man. He proceeded to tell us that he was a professional manager from London. He thought we had talent and he wanted to manage us. Tommy and I told him that we weren't professional, but semi-professionals, and we had families to take care of. We just sat there open-mouthed as he explained to us how he would like us to go down to London to sign a contract at his office, and then go back to work and resign to be fully fledged professional entertainers. He promised us both that we could have far more work than we could ever imagine. Tommy and I were stunned and went back to our table unable to speak, we were floating, it was such a dream come true, like something you only ever read about or see in the movies. We told the lads what he had said and they were very happy for us, so we celebrated by having a few more pints. I went home that night and told Joan, she didn't stand in my way, but I don't think she ever really understood what it meant. The next day, Tommy and I got together and discussed what had taken place the previous night, we decided to give it go, figuring that if it didn't work out we could always go back to welding.

We took a day off work and traveled to London to sign the contract. This was a big day for Tommy and me. We had never before been to London and felt as though we were about to become stars, we signed the contract with no hesitation and had a little look around the capital then set of back to Oldham with our heads in the clouds.

We went to work and told them that we were resigning because we were turning professional. They were very gracious and wished us the best of luck and Tommy and I set off into the largely unknown world of show-business. We had high hopes, but in fact this was going to be the start of the most miserable two years of my life.

Some dreams are meant to be shattered, and our dream was one of those. Our new managers' promise of much work and fame turned out to be hot air. The only work he found for us in twelve months was a weekend in Newcastle. Times began to get hard around this time as we had no work, money was very tight, but Tommy and I decided to stick it out as long as possible to see if we could make it as pro's. Joan was working now, so at least there was a bit of money coming in, but it was barely enough to cover the bills. We argued a lot. But the money didn't seem to matter to me for some reason. I put it all to the back of my mind and hungrily chased my dream.

We began to find small jobs to bring in some cash, like fixing loose slates for someone or building little garden walls. We did anything to survive and worked hard. But after all the efforts, I didn't survive. I was so far behind with my mortgage repayments, that I was now receiving demands from the building society, threatening repossession of the house. That was a time which I will never forget. Here we were, Tommy and I, two so-called professional entertainers, with not a penny in our pockets and not knowing where the next loaf of bread was coming from. We were seated on someone else's roof in the middle of a blizzard putting slates back on for a few quid. I can still see it now. I told Tommy all of my troubles, and said to him how this show-business lark wasn't working out and we should just go back and get a job. I will never forget his optimism. He just listened to me and then told me quietly, with all the confidence in the world, that this was just the start, that we couldn't get any lower than this, and so the only way was up. He managed to take away my fears, and before we knew where we were, we were laughing as though we didn't have a care in the world. All our lives, when things have been rough, Tommy had always tried to keep my spirits up and I thank him for this, because, surely without his confidence and optimism I'm sure I would have given up more than once.

During this struggle, Tommy managed to get a part-time job from a friend of his who had dog kennels. He told me that if I wanted to help him he would give me half his wage. He didn't have to ask twice. Thinking back on it, there was not a lot for me to do there, so I realize that Tommy was just trying to help me out. We used to get to the kennels at around ten o'clock in the morning, clean them out and then spend the rest of the day talking and dreaming about when we would hit the big time. It was not to come for a long time yet and there was to be a lot of heartache along the way. We even went for an audition for a popular television program called 'Opportunity Knocks' and were told that they would be in touch with us. We just knew that had meant we had failed.

Things got so bad that Joan and I approached money lenders to try to get ourselves out of debt. We knew what time the debt collectors would arrive so when they were due to call we would switch off all the lights in the house and hide under the window until they had gone. There were many times when I even had to put my hand over our Roberts' mouth to stop him from shouting at the wrong time. I can still see them now trying to peer through the window to see if we were in. The money lender started to get very nasty, threatening Joan and me that if he didn't get the money, he would take us to court.

We just didn't have it. It didn't bother me too much though, I already had a few court orders against me, what I was worried about was that we were getting more and more behind with the mortgage repayments, and with us having to pay the money lender as well, there was no way I was ever going to get out of the hole that I was in. It was just going deeper and deeper. One day, my sister Sylvia arrived and saw that I was feeling sad. Before long I was blurting out the whole story to her about the money lender and everything. She listened intently and then asked me to tell her what day he came to collect his money. I told her he came on Fridays.

She told me not to worry; everything was going to be alright. Our Sylvia was always like that, nothing ever seemed to worry her. She went through life like a tornado. Friday came and suddenly the doorbell rang. I began to panic; I thought the money-lender had come early. I quickly switched off the lights and darted under the window. Joan and I sat there with our Robert in my arms not daring to breathe. Then I heard our Sylvia calling me from outside.

"Robert, it's me," she shouted.

I let her in, feeling rather stupid, and told her I had thought it was the money-lender who had come early. She didn't say anything, but just laughed. I asked her why she had come and she told me that she had come to see the money-lender. Now I began to worry. I knew our Sylvia would argue with anybody. She calmed my fears and told me that she had a proposition to put to him. I asked her what it was but she wouldn't tell me.

The time came for him to arrive and we all just sat there in silence. Suddenly the door-bell rang and I knew it was him. I let him in, feeling very small. Here was a man with a lot of money who had a hold over me. I felt so humiliated. He came in and just looked at me. I told him that I had no money to pay the debt but if he could give me longer to pay I would give him a pound a week until I had paid it off. He looked at me with disgust and told me in no uncertain terms that this was not good enough. Suddenly, our Sylvia, who up until this point had said nothing, told him that I wasn't going to pay him a pound a week, in fact, she said, I wasn't going to pay him any more of the money that I owed him. There was silence in the room. I thought our Sylvia had lost her mind. The money lender looked at her and demanded to know who she was. She told him that she was my sister and that she had done some checking up on his business. He stood in front of her and told her that he would take me to court and take everything that I owned. Our Sylvia, who stood at only four foot nine, walked across the room to this man and stood in front of him, looking up at him. She told him that she had found out that he was an illegal money-lender and that I had already paid back to him twice the amount that I had borrowed in the first place. She went on to say that she knew he hadn't paid any income tax on his illegal profits, she told him that if he didn't get out of the house now, she would telephone the police and have him arrested for harassment. He turned purple with rage, but there was nothing he could do. Our Sylvia was right. He turned on his heel and left the house, slamming the door and that was the last we ever saw of him. It was amazing that within the space of ten minutes our Sylvia had taken away a nightmare that I thought we would never be rid of. Our Sylvia was always like that, always there whenever we needed her.

My troubles were far from over. The building society was by this time becoming more aggressive about my loan, demanding that I did something regarding the back payments. Joan and I talked it over and decided that it was no use, we would just have to allow them to repossess the house. I wrote them a letter explaining that I couldn't pay and I asked them to take the house from us. They agreed and Joan and I moved into a council house in what was then one of the roughest estates in Oldham. It was called Sholver Estate. Today, after being left derelict and mostly boarded up, Sholver no longer exists, and has been demolished making way for the smart new development now in its place.

In amongst this hard time, one thing happened which brought some sunshine into our lives. We had a second child, another boy with dark hair just like mine. We named him Darren. So now our Robert had a little brother and I was as proud as punch to have two sons.

Things seemed to be looking up all the more as after months of hardship, our career began to take off. We started to get bookings at clubs up and down the country. Ten days in Scotland, ten days in the north-east, ten days in South Wales. Gradually our diary became quite full. The drawback to all this success was that I was spending more and more time away from home, and my marriage began to come apart at the seams. I was so caught up in the excitement of success that I didn't even notice it was crumbling. I'm still surprised that Joan stuck in there as long as she did.

Tommy and I by this time were fully-fledged pro's. We had long since given up the job at the dog kennels and now made our living only by singing. One day Tommy came over to our house very excited. He had just received a letter from a TV program named Opportunity Knocks informing us that we had passed the audition which we had done months ago and they would soon be in touch to tell us when we were to appear on the program. Opportunity Knocks was a TV talent show and many acts from that time began their TV career off the back of that show. This was fantastic news for Tommy and me; we thought that before long we would be stars. What foolish men we were! More would happen to me in the next twelve months of my life than I could have ever conceived.

I went around like a madman telling all my family and

friends that we were going to be on television and that maybe I was going to be a star. They must have thought I was crazy. While my head was in the clouds, my life was crashing down around me. My marriage to Joan was by now non-existent. We didn't ever see one another. She had a job at a factory nearby and during the day I would get Robert and Darren ready for school, and after they finished I would pick them up and make our tea ready for Joan coming home from work. At around six-thirty in the evening Tommy would pick me up and we would travel to clubs all over the place, entertaining. I wouldn't arrive home until the early hours of the morning and by that time Joan would be sound asleep in bed. This went on, day after day, week after week and month after month and whenever we did have time together as a couple, we argued and fought. I was living a lifestyle that just wasn't suited to a marriage and we were both lonely. We found it so hard to be together that it wasn't surprising that we both looked elsewhere for company.

Sometime around then, we had a booking in the North-East for ten days so we gladly packed our bags and went off to make some money, we were ready to escape and have lots of fun. We had just finished working at a club one night when a man came over to us and asked us if we would like to go to a party that he was going to down the road. Would we like to go? Was the man crazy? There was no way he could have stopped us. Before we knew what had happened we were smack bang in the middle of the party. This looked like being a great night. The beer was flowing freely and there were plenty of women about. At this time of my life this was what real life was about, I didn't realize that true happiness came with knowing Jesus, but thankfully, He already had His eye on me.

Suddenly the door burst open and in walked the most beautiful girl I have ever seen. She stood about five foot ten, wearing thigh length boots and a mini skirt. She had the longest legs I have ever seen. Over the top of this she wore an old fur coat which came down to her knees, and her hair was something else. It was dark in a type of page-boy style, but was different as she had one blond streak running all the way down one side of it. In those days this just wasn't done and she stood out like a light-house on a foggy night. With her height she had an air of arrogance about her and she knew that everyone was looking at her. But what gave her away was that she had the saddest eyes I had ever seen. I found out later that the arrogance was a mask for the most loving, gentle person anyone could ever wish to meet.

She was with someone else that night, so I knew that there was no chance for me and besides she was five foot ten and I was five foot four and a quarter, (don't laugh, when you're five foot four, the quarter matters). Tommy and I left the party in the early hours of the morning feeling worse for wear after we'd had too many beers and made our way back to the digs, but it wasn't long before I saw the tall lady again. Two days later we were invited to another party and as Tommy and I were two of the first to arrive, I found myself a comfortable armchair, put a crate of Newcastle Brown Ale beside me and parked myself in it. Now I had my drink and my armchair and I settled back to play my favourite game of people-watching. It doesn't take much energy, but it's amazing what you see, watching how everyone is with each other. The party had been in full swing for about an hour when who should waltz in but my tall lady. This night, she was with a friend. I watched her for about ten minutes, and then decided that tonight I was going to play the game and bring her down a peg or two. Having the only armchair in the place, everyone else was sitting on the floor; I had a great plan to get talking to her.

She was standing just in front of me, so I stood up and tapped her on the shoulder. She turned around and looked down at me. She must have thought, 'Who is this little man' but she didn't say anything. I told her that I was going to the toilet and that she was not to sit in my chair or there would be trouble. I knew that what I had said would ruffle her feathers because I doubted that anyone had ever spoken to her like that before. I went off to the toilet and when I returned, sure enough, she was sitting in my chair. I didn't say anything but just looked at her and to my surprise she got up out of the chair and just smiled at me. I think she knew just what I was up to. She was very charming and told me that her name was Yvonne and that she worked as a waitress at the local nightclub. Maybe she was talking to me out of sympathy, but I didn't care, she was talking to me. Anyway, we spent the rest of the night together, just talking, I hasten to add.

I don't know why, but I went off into some kind of fantasy world. For some reason I told her that I was single, lived alone in a flat in the centre of Oldham and went on telling her so many lies that I began to lose track of what I had said myself. The night passed quickly and before long the dawn arrived. Sadly for me we said our goodbyes and arranged to meet up the following day.

I had been unfaithful to Joan before, but the other women I had been with seemed to be only one-night stands. With Yvonne it was different. I didn't think of anyone else's feelings, only my own. My only worry was whether I would be caught or not.

I met Yvonne a few times during the ten day run in the North-East and really enjoyed her company. She made me feel at ease, the only drawback was the difference in height, she stood much taller than me but it bothered me more than her. On the last night of our run my lies caught up with me. I phoned Yvonne to see if we could meet after our show and she told me in no uncertain terms that it was impossible, because, she said, I had lied to her. I tried to bluff my way out of it but it was no good, she knew. She told me that I had taken her for a fool, and she did not go out with married men. She told me that I should go home and take care of my family instead of going around the country telling lies to everyone, and then she asked me not to ring her again. In my heart I knew she was right but I put the phone down feeling I had lost something very special.

Tommy and I set off for home, and back to reality. After about a week I began to get itchy feet, I wanted to be back on the road. It wasn't too bad, by this time Tommy and I were working on average about three or four times a week. Joan was still at the factory and nothing had changed much, I would mess around all day at home waiting for the boys to finish school and after we'd eaten I'd be off to somewhere with Tommy.

At around this time I noticed that comedians got more money than singers; I never understood why, but now I do. What I learned was that singers can always 'hide' behind a song if things aren't going too well but a comedian has nowhere to hide. I think that's why in those days, a good comedian was paid more than a singer. So one night I dropped in a gag between songs and to my surprise it got a laugh. Now I can tell you, there is no feeling like it in the world when an audience laughs at a joke you have just told. Tommy enjoyed it too. So the next night I did the gag again and it just naturally built up until we were known as comedians. We weren't very good at the beginning, I grant you, but then again to be a comedian is a craft that has to be learned.

Then we received the letter from Opportunity Knocks informing us that we would be appearing in two weeks time. Between the audition and being asked to appear nearly a year had passed and we had by this time moved from being singers to comedians and we had also changed our name from the Harper Brothers to Cannon and Ball. We were now a true comedy double act, with Tommy as the straight man and me as the comic. We felt that Tommy needed a strong name and as he had always liked an American singer named Freddy Cannon, we decided that he should be known as Tommy Cannon. Obviously to make our new name sound like a comedy act I was going to have to be called Ball. It took a lot of persuading on Tommy's part, but eventually I gave in and became Bobby Ball.

One night, around one week before we were due to go to London to record Opportunity Knocks, I was getting ready to go out when the telephone rang. It was our Sylvia. We chatted and she said she wanted to wish me good luck on the show. She went on to tell me that she was feeling very depressed. I talked to her for a while and in the conversation she told me that she felt like taking an overdose of tablets. I wasn't overly worried by this as she had threatened suicide before, many times. She was strong for everyone else but herself. I talked to her and told her I had a gig to do and so I would come to see her in the morning at her house. She was fine with that and she said it was all right and she would see me the next morning. Tommy came to pick me up as usual and we went over to Yorkshire to do a gig. I arrived home at about one o'clock in the morning and was just going to bed when there was a knock at the door. I opened the door and there stood my sister Mavis. Before she could speak I knew exactly what she was going to say.

'Our Sylvia's dead!' I blurted out.

Mavis just looked at me and asked how I knew. I told her about the conversation between me and our Sylvia. Mavis told me not to blame myself as she would have done the same thing. She couldn't ever have known the guilt I felt. It weighed so heavily on my shoulders and preyed on my mind that I could have saved her if only I had gone to her house, I blamed myself, I put show-business before anything else. It was so painful and I cannot describe how deeply the suicide of a loved one affects you. I give thanks to God that much later he came and took my guilt away. I carried it heavily for twenty years and never spoke to a soul about it, but it was always there.

My parents took the death of our Sylvia, their eldest child, very badly. They couldn't understand why she had done it. To them, she had always seemed so bright and cheerful, so self-controlled. What they never knew was that she was always prone to bouts of depression and at that time there were deep personal problems that she couldn't see a way out of. It got too much for her.

The next week I had to go down to London to do Opportunity Knocks. I was on emotional autopilot but I had no choice but to do it. We actually thought we had done reasonably well but we came last in the competition. In fact as a result, we had a few bookings cancelled. As for our dream of making it big, that would have to wait for another fifteen years.

A few short months after all this, my life was again turned upside down. My marriage fell to pieces. It hadn't been good for some time and I knew it was time to do something about it so I decided to leave Joan for a couple of days so that she could see that our marriage was in trouble. I reasoned that if I left, she would come running after me and we could get it all out in the open and work it out. I turned up late one evening on our Mavis's doorstep. She welcomed me in and asked me what the matter was. I proudly told her that I had left Joan to try to teach her a lesson. Our Mavis asked me if I was doing the right thing and I told her yes, because, I thought, Joan would come looking for me after a couple of days and then everything would be alright. Our Mavis lived in a little terraced house. It was a two up, two down with an outside toilet. She told me that the only room she had was the back bedroom and her children slept in that. She said that if I didn't mind sleeping in there with them, I could stay as long as I wanted. It was fine with me. I wouldn't be there very long anyway.

I settled in and waited for Joan to come and get me. One day passed and then another and another. Before long a week had gone by and I had heard nothing. I was beginning to miss her and the kids, so I decided to go back and tell her I was coming home. When I arrived home I found she had changed the locks on the doors, so I broke down the front door and waited for her to come home from work. She eventually arrived back and we sat down to talk out our differences. Joan told me in no uncertain terms that she didn't love me anymore and that she didn't want me to come back. I have never felt so shocked and hurt in my life. I knew we were having some problems, but I never thought in a million years that it was so bad. My mind just wouldn't let me believe what I was hearing. How could she stop loving me just like that? Had I been a bad father? Maybe she didn't mean all these things that she was saying. All these thoughts and more kept rushing around in my brain. Joan explained that the old saying, 'Absence makes the heart grow fonder' wasn't true in her case. With my work taking me all over the country, her love had grown cold and now she wanted me out of her life and wanted to move on.

To separate from or divorce your spouse must be one of the most horrendous things anyone can go through. I felt stripped of my dignity, and felt as though I had failed. The emotional pain is something that unless you've been through it yourself, is impossible to explain. It takes you into a world that you don't understand, there is no security and you begin to feel that you could never possibly smile or love again. I had just lost our Sylvia and now my family had gone. I was an emotional wreck and wished I could die myself.

I went back to our Mavis's, not knowing which way to turn, In my heart I still believed that there might be a chance that she would take me back. I just couldn't stop crying. I went back and made a nuisance of myself, begging her to take me back, all I wanted was my family back and to be there for my two boys. It was not to be, I became a Sunday father. If you look around every Sunday in parks and zoos up and down the country, you will see fathers on their own with their children. I guarantee that half or more of these are Sunday dads who have picked up their children for the day. That was me. I would pick up our Robert and Darren on a Sunday morning and just like so many others, we would go off to the park or something, just so that we could be together. It would break my heart wondering what they thought of me. I wondered if they hated me for not being around, and blamed me for the break up. I wondered if I would lose their love and respect as they grew older. Then I would take them home at the end of the day, hoping that Joan would ask me in.

During these terrible months Tommy would try to keep my spirits up. He would talk to me and tell me that it was about time I got on with my life and stopped looking to the past. But I couldn't see any light at the end of this long black tunnel I was in. Nothing seemed to matter.

We were due to go back to the North-East for another ten day run, so Tommy suggested, to use his words, that I gave 'that tall girl a ring' that I had met twelve months ago and see if I could take her out, because, he said, I had got on well with her before.

I told him she wouldn't go out with me because she had found out that I was married, and that she didn't like me anymore because I had lied to her. Besides, I wasn't sure if she would remember me or not. He told me to stop being so negative and at least give it a try.

'Who knows', he said, 'She might make you laugh again'.

We arrived in the North-East, got settled into the digs and then after much thought I plucked up the courage to ring her. I could hear it ringing at the other end and my heart was thumping as if it was going to jump out of my chest. Eventually she answered.

'Hello?'

It was good to hear her voice. All the memories of the few days we spent together came flooding back to me.

'Hello,' I eventually replied.

'Who is it?'

It took me quite a while to answer. I wasn't sure whether she would put the phone down or not.

'It's me, Bobby Harper.'

The line went silent for a moment, and I could tell that she couldn't remember me, or she was pretending not to. I decided to help her remember.

'You know', I said, 'Bobby Harper. You'll remember me as one of the Harper Brothers.'

'Oh yes!' she said, as though my name had just connected with her memory cells. 'That little man who tells lies.'

It was obvious that she hadn't forgotten. I tried to smooth things over.

'Yes,' I answered quickly. 'I was just wondering', I continued, 'you see, I am working up here for a few days and I was wondering if you would like to go out for a meal or something?'

'I told you before; I don't go out with married men.' She replied, very tersely.

So that was my answer. There was no way she was going to go out with me. But, true to form, I wasn't about to give up, I didn't want to let her get away this time.

'But I'm not married now,' I said. 'Well, I am married, but we've split up, I'm separated.'

It hadn't come out quite as smooth as I had wanted, but at least it was the truth. The line went quiet for a while and I could almost hear her brain working. She must have been able to tell that I was being honest with her because to my surprise she said,

'Okay then, I will meet you in the town about eight o'clock.'

I put the phone down a bit stunned, then for the first time in many months I felt happiness. I didn't know whether she had agreed to meet me because she liked me or because she felt sorry for me, but it didn't matter, at least she was meeting me.

That evening I met her and took her to a restaurant, after seeing the prices on the menu I realized that I only had enough money for one meal, I asked her what she would like and was so relieved when she told me that she didn't want anything, it was quite late and she wasn't hungry. I ordered myself a mixed grill but couldn't eat it as I was so nervous. We got talking and I explained what had happened, and she just sat there and listened while I poured my heart out. When I had finished my tale of woe she just took my hand and told me that everything was going to be alright.

We got on like a house on fire and saw each other every night after that. When it came time for me to leave the North-East and go back home, we found that we couldn't be apart. So that is when we started what I call my 'two-hundred mile courtship'. From then on four times a week I would drive from Oldham to Stockton-on-Tees, a round trip of two hundred miles. It was worth every minute on the road. As Tommy had predicted, she taught me to laugh again.

Our career was really starting to take off. We were now doing the nightclub circuit and we were going down well wherever we went. I remember one club we went to in Leeds, one of many, Tommy and I had a double that night, meaning we had to do two clubs on the same night, it was New Years Eve and we were both a little bit worse for wear as we had already partaken in the festivities. It was around eleven o'clock by the time we had arrived at the second club and as we went in the back door, we saw a long dark corridor leading to the stage.

There in front of us was a figure of a man, dressed in a top hat and cape. He was just about to go on, when I thought I would be friendly and wish him a happy new year, so I ran up to him and slapped him on the back.

'Happy New Year!' I said with a huge grin on my face.

His head shot round and he looked at me as though he wanted to kill me, I didn't understand, I was only being friendly. He didn't have time to say anything to me as he had just been announced by the compare and was already making his way on stage. I realized then why he had looked at me in that way. When I slapped him on the back I hadn't known that he was a magician. It was only when I saw a few birds feathers fall from beneath his cloak as he walked on stage that I realized I had hit one of the birds hidden within his cloak. I just stood there watching with a macabre sense of humour for a bird with a broken wing or even worse, a dead one to fall out from under his cloak. But I was spared; they all seemed to be okay. I did learn a valuable lesson, however, never again would I go near anyone who was about to go on stage.

Another time I took Yvonne to a social club where Tommy and I were working that night. On the show was a guitar vocalist. We had just sat down when the concert chairman came over and told us to get ready because we were going on first. We went into the dressing room and told him that we were comedians and comedians, as a rule in show business, did not open the show. He didn't appreciate our giving him advice and told us in no uncertain terms that it was his decision and we were going on first. Tommy and I were, by now, quite used to social clubs and people like him, who, when they got their badge became power mad, so we knew it would be a waste of time trying to change his mind. He was the boss and in his mind he knew much more about show-business than we did. He left us looking at one another open-mouthed in the dressing room. We resigned ourselves to the fact that we would be going on first and proceeded to get changed and ready. We had just taken off our trousers when he came back.

'No!' he said, in his broad North East accent. 'I've decided you are perfectly right. I'm putting the guitar-vocalist on first.'

He gave us a smile and left. Tommy and I looked at each other and decided that maybe he wasn't so bad after all. We put our trousers back on and joined Yvonne at our table. She asked us what was wrong and I explained that the concert chairman had changed his mind and he didn't know what he was doing but every-thing was alright now. We had been sitting there for about five minutes when he came back.

'No!' he said, 'I was right the first time. You two will have to go on first.'

Tommy and I got up like two schoolchildren and made our way back to the dressing room. We had just taken off our trousers for the second time when he burst in.

'I've been thinking,' he said, 'maybe you were right. The guitar-vocalist can go on first.'

Tommy opened his mouth to speak but the man stopped him.

'Don't argue with me lad,' he said, 'I've made up my mind and that's final!'

Tommy and I put on our trousers again and joined Yvonne again. This routine of coming and telling us we were on first and then coming and then we weren't, went on for quite a while. After the fourth time Tommy and me were becoming very annoyed. He approached us for the fifth time and told us that no, we were going on first. We went into the dressing room and were just about to take our trousers off again when he came in.

'Hold it!' he said, 'the guitar-vocalist has just told me that he doesn't mind going on first, so, that's what we'll do.'

'Is it?' Tommy said. He was very angry by this time. 'Well, I'll tell you what we will do,' he continued, 'my friend Bobby and I are not going on at all tonight, so you and your friend the guitar-vocalist can entertain this audience by yourselves.'

Tommy began to pack our things away and the concert chairman just looked at me dumbfounded.

'What does he mean?' He said to me when he had eventually found his voice.

'He means,' I said, relishing the moment, 'that *you* can go on first, and then *you* can put the guitar vocalist on, because *we* won't be here.'

He stared at us as if we had gone mad. It was obvious that nobody had ever spoken to him like that before, especially an act; who were generally treated like vermin.

'Are you saying that you are refusing to go on?' he asked, blinking nervously,

Tommy looked up from what he was doing and said,

'That is exactly what we mean. You can take your money and your club and shove it where the sun doesn't shine.'

Tommy always did have a nice way of phrasing things.

'You can't do that' the concert chairman said, his voice getting louder.

'Can't we?' answered Tommy, who by this time had the bit between his teeth, 'just watch us. Come on Bobby.'

We walked out of the dressing-room and started to make our way through the packed out club. The concert chairman came running after us like a man possessed, arms flailing.

'You'll never work in show-business again,' he shouted after us, 'I will report you to the agent.'

Tommy and I just turned around and smiled at him. This infuriated him even more.

'I'll tell every club in the North-East,' he shouted, 'you won't work around here again.'

By this time all the people in the club were looking at us. When they realized what was happening, they started to turn nasty.

'Get out! We don't want you in the club,' a few began to shout, but Tommy and I kept on smiling. Suddenly I realized that we were walking down the opposite side of the club to where Yvonne was sitting. I looked across at her and could see she was wondering what on earth was happening.

'Come on love' I shouted across the room, 'we're going to a proper club.'

This sent the crowd into a rage, but somehow we managed to get out. Once outside, I told Yvonne what we had said to the concert chairman and she laughed like I'd never seen her laugh before. I realized then that not only was she a woman whom I found very attractive, but she was also my soul mate. Anyway we all went down the street laughing and headed for the Fiesta club, where Yvonne had worked, to have some fun.

I remember when I first met Yvonne's parents. Tommy and I were doing a social club one night and I arranged to meet Yvonne outside her house after the gig and we would go from there to the Fiesta Club. When we finished the gig, I arrived at her house only to find her standing at the window. She beckoned to me to go in so I assumed her parents must be out. I went inside and she told me that she wasn't quite ready so I sat down on the couch to wait for her. Just then the door opened and in walked her mother, she looked at me and I stood up and shook her hand. I was feeling very embarrassed, I was taken back to when I was a teenager again on his first date. We politely said our hello's and then she asked Yvonne if she could see her for a couple of minutes in the kitchen and I wondered if I was going to be thrown out of the house at any moment. After a while Yvonne returned and we left. When we got outside I asked her what her mother had said. Yvonne told me that her mother had seen my dark hair and skin and asked if I was Pakistani, she also wondered why on earth Yvonne wanted to go out with such a short man. Yvonne let her know that I am in fact English and that I am the tallest in my family.

Yvonne and I made up our minds and decided to marry. But I had a problem, I had to tell Yvonne that I had absolutely no money and if she still wanted to marry me it would mean living at our Mavis's house in the back bedroom with her two children! She told me she wasn't bothered as long as we could be together. Up until that time, Yvonne hadn't met any of my family, so she decided one weekend that she would travel down to Shaw and meet everyone. Yvonne met our Mavis and they became firm friends almost immediately. I think our Mavis was pleased to see that Yvonne had brought some happiness into my life after seeing all the pain I had gone through. The next thing I had to do was take Yvonne to my parent's house and introduce her to them. She was petrified; she felt like she was taking Joan's place as she had heard how my mother and father had liked Joan so by the time we reached the house it took me a few moments to coax her out of the car. I introduced her to them as the girl I was going to marry, and my mother made a great fuss of her and commented on 'what a bonny lass' she was. My father didn't say much, but just kept looking at her. Eventually I asked him what he thought. He carried on looking at her and with a twinkle in his eye said,

'She's tall, isn't she?

'Yes,' I replied, 'What do you think of her' I was feeling proud now as I could tell that he liked her.

'She'll be alright for cleaning the windows,' he said.

Yvonne laughed, but I could see a strange look in her eyes. When we got outside, I asked her if she was okay.

'Don't think I'm being funny Bob', she said, 'but I didn't understand a word your Dad said.'

'Why did you laugh then?' I asked, I was confused,

'Because they might have thought I was ignorant if I didn't,' she replied, still a bit worried. Now it was my turn to laugh. I realized that she couldn't understand my Father because he spoke in such a broad Lancashire accent, and as Yvonne came from the North-East it was a whole new language to her.

Yvonne and I got married on January 16th at the Oldham registry office and it was the biggest fiasco I have ever seen. The problem is that when I get nervous, I start to laugh and it is a problem that lands me in more trouble than I care to talk about. I have even been known to burst out laughing at funerals. But this time was the worst of all. It had been a monumental struggle for us to get to this point. With one problem after another, making us wait for our big day. We stood in front of the registrar, Yvonne and I, with Tommy as my best man and all our guests standing behind us. The registrar was reading out the wedding vows and I felt a laugh rising up from my belly. It was unbelievable, I could feel it starting and tried my best to suppress it but it was no good. What made it worse was that Tommy could tell just by looking at me and as laughter is highly contagious he had caught my eye and started to snigger. I have never felt so embarrassed in my life. I didn't want to laugh, but I couldn't help it. The registrar was giving Tommy and me funny looks, but the more he did that, the more we laughed. I didn't want to ruin Yvonne's big day and certainly didn't want her to think I was laughing because I was marrying her. But my fears were unfounded because suddenly I could see Yvonne out of the corner of my eye beginning to giggle beside me. She had caught the laughing bug too. Before long it had spread around half of the guests who also were trying their utmost to suppress their laughter. After what seemed like an age, the registrar finally announced us as man and wife and I am quite sure he must have been glad to see the back of us. He must have thought we were crazy. We must have been, because Yvonne and I had decided to get married on a day when I was working, and not only was I working, but I was doing two clubs that night. So it was arranged that Yvonne and all the guests would go to the second club, while Tommy and I would do the first club and meet them later at the second club after we had done our spot. Tommy and I arrived at the second club and saw all my wedding party waiting for me. We did our spot and joined them but it was a very strange feeling being on stage and seeing my own wedding party in the audience; it felt as though Tommy and I were the cabaret act booked for the wedding. At the end of the night Yvonne and I went on 'honeymoon'; one night at the Royal George Hotel in Rochdale, which was the next town, four miles away.

We had our one night alone in Rochdale and then traveled back to our Mavis's and the back bedroom with the kids. It was so gracious of our Mavis and Trevor to take us in like that. It was only a tiny house and we are still so grateful for all the kindness they showed towards us. We grew so well as a family and got on so well that instead of arguments and tensions arising from there being so many in such a confined space, a strong bond was created that has never been broken.

The back bedroom was so tiny that all we could fit in there was a single bed. As Yvonne and I had no money, we had to make do, so we slept on that single bed which was raised from the floor by four house bricks. Also in the room were the bunk beds where the children slept. One night I lay there with my arms around Yvonne thinking of the future. I could hear the children sleeping deeply in the quietness of the night. I could tell that Yvonne wasn't asleep. I could almost hear her thinking also about what her future held.

I lay there thinking deep into the night, about how my life had turned out, about my two boys, oh, I thought a lot about my two boys, about Yvonne, how she had given up her life to come and live with me, who had no money and no future; how she had left her family a hundred miles away to come and live with me in a back bedroom of someone else's terraced house, in a place where she had no friends of her own. I felt an overwhelming sense of hopelessness. As I lay there wallowing in self pity, a different feeling began to overcome it, a feeling of confidence. At that time I didn't know what it was; now I am certain it was the Lord, telling me that everything was going to be alright.

I whispered Yvonne's name, she turned to face me and I took hold of her hand. I told her that everything was going to be alright. I told her that some day, I would buy her a big house and that she would have more clothes than she would know what to do with. I said that one day, we would have a Rolls Royce. She smiled and just patted my hand and told me maternally not to worry and get some sleep. I understood, she thought I was dreaming. I wasn't. I knew that all the things I had just said would come true, and they did. What I didn't know was the pain that all these things would bring with them, but it would all be in the Lord's plan on my journey to meeting Him.

Chapter 5

The Man from Oxfam

On May 15th 1972, Yvonne presented me with a baby, a girl. We named her Joanne. Now my family was complete, I had two sons and a daughter. I continued to see the boys each Sunday and they were growing up into two fine lads.

By this time my career with Tommy was doing very well. We were out working nearly every night and had started to make better money. Now Yvonne and I could begin to think about getting a place of our own. We had a lot of difficulty in this area, we could find houses we liked, but we couldn't get a mortgage because the Building Societies classed show business as a risk. It's funny, but when you become a 'star', you are no longer classed as a risk. So we went into rented property and as we had no furniture of our own, we had to get somewhere that was already furnished. We eventually found a house and settled in. It was great. Now we were a real family with space of our own.

Things were going great for Tommy and me. We now had a manager, a man named Stuart Littlewood. He had managed us previously but had sacked us for not turning up at gigs. We had a second chance with him now as long as we promised to behave ourselves and work anywhere he had booked us. We told him we would and that our wild days were over. If only he knew, they were only just beginning.

One day in 1973, he telephoned us to let us know that he had got us a summer season at the Carlton Hotel on the island of Guernsey. This was our first ever summer season, which would mean us working at the seaside resort for the duration of the summer, we would be resident there and this would mean we wouldn't have to keep traveling up and down the country. A summer season could mean at least twenty weeks solid work, and so as you can imagine, we were very excited when we heard this news.

The weeks seemed to pass very slowly until the summer came, but eventually we set off. Yvonne and I rented a house on the island and when we arrived we found it was such a big place that Tommy could have the downstairs and we would have the upstairs and we would share the kitchen. When we were all settled in Tommy and I headed for the Carlton Hotel to see where we would be working. To our delight we found that it was a properly produced show with other acts and dancers. This was quite new to Tommy and me. We felt that after all this time we were now really in show business. On the bill was a magician named Sonny Neil and a singing trio called the Song Spinners. Topping the bill was a tenor singer by the name of Kevin Ross and of course there was Tommy and Me. Oh and I mustn't forget the dancers.

This was going to be exciting. The season started and Tommy and I were the second act on after the magician. We were doing alright, until one day when Harry, one of the Song Spinners, got talking. He told me that I really couldn't call myself a comic because we sang quite a lot of songs. In those days Tommy and I would wear two nice suits and do about two minutes cross patter between songs. I couldn't stop thinking about what he said and I asked him to explain what he had said and what we could do about it. He told me that to be a real comic I should do something which would make the audience sit up and take notice from the minute we walked on stage. He even suggested that I should even make my entrance from the audience. I realized that Harry was right. To be different from other comics I knew that we had to do something quite outrageous.

I worked on the idea and decided to make my entrance from the audience as an autograph hunter, wanting Tommy's autograph. The first thing I had to do was to ditch my nice, safe, stage suit and buy something which would make people look at me. I told Tommy my idea and he agreed that we should try it. The next day we went into the town centre and were just passing the Oxfam shop when I spotted the ideal thing in the window. It was an oversized black evening suit. It would have fit a twenty-stone man. It was much too large for me but it was ideal. Tommy and I went into the shop and the salesman looked at me as though I had lost my mind when I said I would like to try it on. I went into the changing room and put on the suit. As soon as I had it on I knew I had found the real Bobby Ball. It felt good, I felt like a comic. It made me feel funny. I walked out of the changing room and Tommy burst out laughing. I knew then that it was right. He explained what had made him laugh. It was the pants, which were so long that they hung in folds around my shoes. While we were in there, we bought a large blue cummerbund, and the only other thing I needed now were shoes. I spotted some old Hush Puppy boots in the corner so I said I would take them as well. Now I was ready. At last we had found me a character.

The evening came and we decided to try it out. Nothing like this was being done in show business at that time so it was quite a new thing to do. I was going to make my entrance from the audience as an autograph hunter, which would mean I would have to sit in the audience before the show started. The room that we were working in was small, with tables and chairs spread around in front of the stage where people would watch the show and drink. Just before the show began I changed into my new stage clothes and walked around to the front of the hotel. I could see all of the people walking in and my nerve began to go. There was no turning back now, I had come so far. There I was, a little man in a huge baggy suit, my black curly hair parted down the middle, with brown hush puppy boots on. To make myself look even more ridiculous I had an old 'Brownie' camera hanging around my neck. I reasoned that no autograph hunter worth his salt would be seen without his camera. I began to have second thoughts; this wasn't the show business I had been brought up to imagine. To me, show-business was all sequins and glitz, and look at me, totally the opposite. I took a very deep breath and prepared to 'die the death' (a term used when the audience don't like you.) I began to walk towards the crowd of people going into the show and I knew that my adrenalin was working overtime because my bottom had gone tight! Before I knew it I was in amongst them and started to act as though I was one of them. I noticed people looking at me strangely. It felt quite good because I knew this idea might just have a chance of working. I went into the room, found a table and sat down. I waited for the show to begin. People were looking at me from across the room. They thought I was somebody who wasn't a 'full shilling'. I loved it and began to play my role to the full, ordering drinks from the waiters and coughing loudly. I had a table to myself because everyone avoided sitting near me, this was understandable.

I sat there for a while and wondered if the whole idea had been a mistake, when suddenly the lights went down and the curtains opened. The audience now lost interest in me and settled back to enjoy the show. In fact, I started to enjoy it myself, it was the first time I had seen it from the audience's point of view. The dancers came on and then the magician. Then a voice boomed out from the back of the stage and announced Tommy Cannon. I started to sweat, it was now or never. Tommy came on and began to sing his song. I let him get into about one line of the song and then I started to shout as loud as I could for his autograph, he ignored me and so I stood up and made my way to the stage, still shouting. Tommy stopped singing and there was a deathly hush. The people believed that I was some kind of crackpot who was ruining the show. I climbed on stage with Tommy and looked at the audience. You could have heard a pin drop. They were staring at me with their mouths wide open. The sweat started to roll down my back. Tommy and I went into the routine we had rehearsed.

I can understand the audience for not laughing at the autograph routine, nor would I expect them to; that was for the shock factor, but for us this was original material. The routine would go like this; Tommy would be on stage acting as though he were a solo performer, then I would come out of the audience, dressed in my ill-fitting suit, pretending that Tommy was my hero. I would ask, or rather, shout for his autograph which Tommy would impatiently give me, hoping that I would leave the stage and all the time I would be chattering, saying things like:

'You are my favourite, Tommy, I've got all your record!' or 'You're a leg-end to me Tommy.'

Surprisingly these little sayings used to get lots of laughs and so we kept them in and expanded it. Later on in our career the routine would sometimes backfire on us because we eventually did it too well. I would sometimes even be thrown out of clubs because people would complain that I was a nuisance and they wanted to watch Tommy. They actually did think that I was an autograph hunter, but once it became clear that I was part of the act they would feel silly and of course the routine went down much better once this happened.

It seemed as though we had been up there for a thousand years before someone somewhere at the back of the room started to laugh. To this day I thank God for that one person who began to laugh. Before long the entire audience was laughing loudly and it felt wonderful. We came off and looked at one another, we were on a high. We knew that we had just done something totally original and not just a copy of all the other double acts. That night we became the Cannon and Ball act which would eventually bring us success.

We were having a great time that summer, we had a new act and my two boys Robert and Darren had joined us for a two-week holiday. Yvonne and I decided that we needed a car get us around the island, but we didn't have that kind of money so it was out of the question, until a friend said he knew where there was an old banger for sale at twenty-five quid. I told Yvonne about it and she said she would manage without her housekeeping money for a week so that I could have the car. I rushed around to the address where the car was for sale, very excited, only to find that it was a clapped-out Ford Prefect. But that didn't deter me. I wanted a car, whatever state it was in. I asked the man if he would take any less for the car, but he was adamant on the price, and with me not being the best person at bartering I paid him the asking price for the car and drove it away. On the way home I knew I had bought trouble because when I looked in my rear view mirror I couldn't see any cars behind me for the smoke. There was so much smoke coming from my exhaust the car looked like a moving bonfire. It also didn't like hills. I knew it didn't because it refused to go up them. Whenever I came to a hill I had to get out and get someone to help me push it up. But it didn't matter because I loved that car. It had character. It was a car that I think back on with fond memories. When

I got home I showed my new car off to Yvonne with pride in my heart. She looked at it and the look in here eyes said it all. She knew I had been conned, but true to Yvonne's character, she just smiled and said that if I was happy then that's all that mattered.

One day Yvonne was busy cleaning the house and I was busy doing nothing as usual, and the kids were getting very bored so I decided it was about time that Ethel (that's what I had named my car) had a new coat of paint. Funnily enough I had found some old tins of paint when I had been rummaging about in the garage at the back of the house so I knew it would cost us much money for Ethel to look spick and span. I had a plan, so I got all the kids together (Tommy's and mine), and asked them to pick a colour each. They looked at the tins of red and blue and yellow paint and their little eyes lit up. I told them that as they had been good children they could paint the car. They all let out screams of excitement, but I told them that I didn't want it painted like any ordinary car, because this was a special car. I wanted it painted in pictures. I told them they could paint whatever pictures came into their minds. As I was telling them I watch as their eyes opened wider and wider as their imaginations took flight. I gave them all a brush and a tin of paint and told them to let me know when they had done and with screams of excitement they ran out of the door towards Ethel.

After about two hours our Robert came in covered in red paint. He just looked at me with the face of a dirty angel.

"We've finished dad" he said, over-acting as if he was out of breath from all the hard work, "Do you want to look at Ethel."

Did I? Hitler's army couldn't have stopped looking at what they had done. I shouted to all the adults to follow me outside. When we got out side Yvonne, Tommy and I just couldn't stop laughing. There stood all the kids covered from head to toe in paint, grinning back at us. But what made us laugh more was what they had done to Ethel. She stood there looking like something out of a nursery. She was covered in childish paintings. They written their names all over her and there were pictures of clowns, dogs, cats anything and everything a child would paint. To my eyes she looked wonderful. I told the children they had done a great job and gave them ten pence each. At least it had passed an afternoon for them. That night as I drove to the hotel I could see everybody turning open-mouthed to watch as this back-firing, smoke-belching, multi-coloured machine come down the street. I couldn't help but laugh to myself, knowing that no one had ever seen anything like this before on this sedate island of Guernsey. Ethel managed to cough and splutter her way through the season, and then a week before the season ended she coughed her last and died.

Disaster struck around three-quarters of the way through the season. I received a letter from the Inland Revenue which stated that I owed them a substantial amount of money, money I just didn't have. Yvonne and I were devastated. We had only just managed to get on our feet and felt we had got over the worst and now here I was heading back again to rock bottom. We talked it over and realized that there was no way we would be able to pay them. Yvonne got serious, and took control as usual. She sat me down on the couch, and holding my hands in hers explained that after the summer season we would have to split up. This was harrowing news and I didn't know what to do. Before my eyes my new family was disintegrating. Oh, I was fine when it came to going on stage and showing myself off, but when it came to real life I was hopeless. She must have seen the panic in my eyes, because she quickly told me not to worry, it wouldn't be permanent. She would get her job back at home and live with her parents, while I would go back

My Mam & Dad

My Mam

Right toe

Winding up the Nolans

With Albert Finney

On stage

Panto

Have fun in panto

With two mates, Stu Francis
& Graham Grumbleweed

I loved this bike

Darren & Robert

Darren & Robert, two chips
off the old block

With my sons

Yvonne and me

Holidaying with Joanne and
three of our grandchildren

My Grandchildren

Tom and me in the Bush
Telegraph

Jungle Gnome

In trouble in the jungle

Cooking up mischief in the jungle

to our Mavis's and by doing this we could save all the money we earned and pay off our debts. I loved her, the way she said, 'our debts' when she should have said, 'your debts'. I could see that what she was saying was that this was the only way out of the mess I had got us into, so I unwillingly agreed. I wrote to the Inland Revenue and detailed just how much I could afford to pay back each week and thankfully they agreed to the amount I had given. Yvonne and I got through the rest of the season, but it wasn't the same as before, there was now an air of insecurity in our relationship.

The season ended at the end of September and my daughter Joanne went with Yvonne back to her parents' house in the North-East. I went back to the 'ever faithful', our Mavis's. It was a terrible feeling going back there alone. It felt as though I was starting all over again. But every week whatever money I had earned, I would take up to Yvonne and she would put her wage and my wage together and whatever we had left after living expenses, she would use to pay my debts off. Eventually, after a long three months, she managed to straighten me out and for the first time in my adult life, I had absolutely no debts.

Now that I was in the clear it was time to get my family back together and start again. We rented another furnished house and Yvonne came back to join me again in Oldham. It felt wonderful to see my wife and daughter again, to get up in the mornings and they were there. I made a vow to myself that we would never split up again, but with the nature of work I was in, this proved impossible.

I thought it was great to be living in a rented house, with no worry about mortgages and debts, but I could see that Yvonne wanted a house of her own. She knew it was difficult to get a mortgage with me being in show business, so she kept this dream to herself and we just kept moving from rented house to rented house. One day we visited my mother and father and across the road, in what used to be the fields I had once played in, a building firm had took over and work was beginning on a new housing estate. On a huge billboard in front of the site, the houses were advertised for sale at £7000 each. This was pretty cheap for a brand new house in those days, and Yvonne was quick to point this out. She also pointed out that it was about time that we had a home of our own. I argued with her that we were fine as we were; I told her I didn't need the worry of a mortgage. I'd been there and done that. She reasoned with me that instead of paying rent to a stranger to pay off *their* mortgage, we might as well use the payments to pay for our own property. I agreed with her and asked her to find out what the deposit was on the property. I thought that would keep her quiet because I knew that we didn't have enough money for a deposit. But I underestimated my wife's determination. She went out to the contractor's office to find out all the details. I could tell by the look in her eyes that she was excited. She sat down and told me that there would be no problem about me getting the mortgage, they would sort all that out, and also the deposit was only £100. After she told me all her exciting news she sat there, looking at me expectantly. How could I refuse? She was the one who had given up everything and gone back home so that we could pay my debts off. I looked deep into her soft brown eyes, and they looked back at me, pleading. There was no way I could have refused that woman. I told her that I was willing to go for it if she was. She squealed with delight and gave me the biggest hug I have ever had in my life. This was to be the start of the fall and rise of Bobby Harper.

It was 1976, and 29 Harewood Road was the address of our new home. The contractor had shown us around and we were very excited. It was a three-bedroom, semi-detached house with gardens, back and front. It was our first home. We didn't have any furniture, but to us this was a minor problem. At last we had our own house. It was to be a further two months before we move in as the builders hadn't finished the road and gardens yet, but that didn't matter. Yvonne and I had all the time in the world.

Cannon and Ball were doing pretty well by this time too. We had regular bookings and everything was going great. One day, our manager phoned to tell us he had got us six-weeks in none other than Australia and we were to leave in one month. He gave us the date and it meant that I would be away when Yvonne and I were due to move into our new house. On one hand, I was very excited at going away, as neither me or Tommy had ever been abroad before, and on the other hand I was very worried about telling Yvonne because I knew how disappointed she would be, she was looking forward to the move.

I plucked up the courage to tell her that we would have to change our moving date as I wouldn't be there but she was adamant that we were moving on the arranged date, there was no budging her, she had waiting so long. I told her that I couldn't get out of the Australia gig and she said it was fine for me to go; she could do all the moving herself. So that was that.

On the morning that I was due to leave for Australia I kissed Yvonne goodbye in the morning and set off to meet Tommy at the airport. It was a wonderful experience. There we were, two ex-welders from Oldham, boarding a huge 747 to take us to the other side of the world on our first journey abroad. I sat back in my seat as the huge plane took off into the sky and watched as the ground below slowly disappeared. It gave me such a strange feeling. I was stepping into the unknown. It was brilliant. I sat there thinking of Yvonne and the children and as we left they slowly drifted to somewhere at the back of my mind and they were replaced with thoughts of the future. During the flight Tommy and I were like two children in Disney World. We had never been in a large aircraft before, so things like 'in-flight' movies and trolleys full of free drinks were new to us. I have to tell you, we felt like a million dollars.

We landed, eventually, in Sydney, and the agent from that end met us at the airport. He drove us to our hotel and informed us that we had three days off before we would be working. This meant that we had three days to enjoy ourselves. We bade the agent a jolly farewell and walked into our hotel. We asked for the keys to our rooms and he told us in his nicest voice that he only had one room booked for us. We didn't want to cause a fuss so we told him that would be quite adequate. He showed us to our room and when we saw it we couldn't believe our eyes. Outside the hotel had looked very nice but inside it was a different kettle of fish. The room was small and in the corner stood a two-ring gas stove, thickly covered in grease, (the porter explained that the hotel had no restaurant or room-service and if we wanted food, we would have to make it ourselves.) The room had two single beds and over them were two, almost black, mosquito nets, which, judging by the colour of them, they hadn't been washed since the day the hotel had bought them. It felt like I was on the set of an old B-movie set in the Amazon rain forest. At any moment I expected a mean white hunter to burst in. I was not that lucky. Standing against one wall was an old wardrobe that had seen better days; looking at it, I was almost frightened to hang my clothes in it. Hanging on the other wall was an old cupboard with paint peeling off it. This was for our food, the porter happily told us, when we had bought some. Tommy and I just looked at each other and agreed silently that there would be no chance of that. There was an old smelly carpet on the floor, full of holes.

We asked the porter whereabouts we were situated

here in Sydney and he smiled and with a knowing wink said we were in Kings Cross. We didn't have a clue what he meant but it wasn't long before we found out. Our hotel was slap bang in the centre of Sydney's red-light district. It had an ominous reputation all over the world. Tommy and I were from the back streets of Oldham and obviously had never heard of it before. The porter just stood there, with his slimiest 'I can get you anything you want' look on his face, wanting his tip. When we didn't he turned on his heel and with a curt, 'good-day' and left. He didn't even bid us an enjoyable stay. He just left, slamming the door behind him.

Tommy and I were dumbfounded. We just stood there. What had we got ourselves into? We threw our suitcases on the beds and sat down. We just looked at each other and started to laugh. Here we were in the centre of Sydney, the sun was shining outside, (not that we could see it through the grimy windows), we were alone on the other side of the world and we had an adventure before us; and we felt upset because we didn't have a nice room. We weren't even paying for it! We laughed at the absurdity of it all and decided we should unpack our clothes. As we were unpacking I thought I saw something move under Tommy's bed. I looked again, but couldn't see anything, so I didn't say anything and put it to the back of my mind, thinking it must have been my imagination. After we had unpacked, we lay on the beds and began to plan what we would do that night. For some reason I got up and began to have a look around, I opened the cupboard that was hanging on the wall. I opened the doors and jumped back, horrified at what I saw. There, crawling about inside were dozens and dozens of cockroaches. I shouted to Tommy and he ran across to see, my skin began to crawl as I had never seen a cockroach before. Then I remembered before when I thought I'd seen something under Tommy's bed. I told him and we moved the bed to have a look. I had been right; there were more under the beds, crawling all over one another to escape. I hated them, they made my feel dirty! Tommy handled it much better that I could. Right away we went out and bought some cockroach killer. We sprayed around the room and then went out to have a look around the shops while the spray did its job. When we got back, all the cockroaches were dead, so we got to work and swept them all up. But for the rest of our six weeks there, I couldn't go to sleep until I had checked that Tommy and I were alone.

We had a great time in Australia and as the people were so friendly we got to know them quite quickly. So the six weeks became a routine of lying in the sun all day and partying after work all night. I soon became accustomed to this way of life, and the more comfortable I was, living like this, the further Yvonne and kids slipped to the back of my mind. Money was a little tight; I would get about £50 a week, so I'd send Yvonne £12 and keep the rest for myself. Occasionally I would wonder about how she was making ends meet, but I didn't worry too much as I was caught up in the 'me first before anyone else' syndrome.

On our final weekend before we were due to fly home, the agent told us he had organized two concerts for four acts to entertain at a club in a mining town in the middle of the bush. It was arranged that we would all fly out in a small plane to the town, do the two shows and fly back again. The plane was so small that we all sat there facing one another. On the journey with us were another double act called McNeal and Trotter, a comedian called Mike Harris, and woman singer named Ramona. We already knew the double act and the comedian, but we didn't know the woman, and, as it was going to be a long weekend I decided I wasn't going to be lonely. So as soon as we had said our hellos and settled down for the flight, I started to chat to the woman before anyone else could. She was in her late thirties and had an air of pomposity about her. She was striking to look at, and had a great figure. She was a little old for me at the time, but I reasoned to myself that beggars couldn't be choosers. Up until now she had ignored every one of us, but I thought that was maybe because she was shy. She just sat there looking out of the window as though we didn't exist. It was time to make my move.

I said hello, and she turned silently to look at me and then turned to look out of the window again. Well, I wasn't the type of person to be put off with a simple rebuff, so I tried again. I asked her what her name was. She turned once again and looked at me as though I was dirt under her feet, 'Ramona' she replied. She then turned away and looked out of the window again. This was getting beyond a joke. Tommy and all the others had by now stopped talking and were watching this little saga unfold before their eyes. Well, how could I stop now, I was going to get her to say more than one word to me if it killed me so I asked her what kind of act she did, did she sing ballads or pop songs? I must have asked the right question because she slowly turned away from the window, raised one eyebrow and looked at me. I felt like trapped prey.

'I,' she said haughtily, 'do not sing ballads, or pop songs. I am a contralto singer. I am classically trained so therefore I sing classical music. And so,' she added, 'I do not usually mix with variety acts.'

With that she turned back towards the window leaving me to sink further into my sink. This must have interested Tommy, because he started to try to talk to her. He got no further than I did, receiving only one word answers to all of his questions.

He gave up, eventually, and one by one all of the other boys tried, but they each received the same treatment so we left her alone.

When we arrived at the mining town I was amazed. It was as though I had just stepped into a cowboy film. It had one main dirt street, (which must have turned into a quagmire when it rained), and a boardwalk with little shops running alongside it. We booked into a little rickety hotel and spent the rest of the time sleeping until it was time to go to the club. On arrival at the club we were met by a huge Australian miner who told us that he was in charge. He informed us that show we were to do that night was a stag show, men only, and then the following night it would be mixed. We all said okay and then went to the dressing rooms to get ourselves ready. The club began to fill up and I took a peek through the curtains. Just looking made me sweat. The room was full of big Australian miners, some of whom had obviously come direct from work and hadn't even been home to change and wash. I could tell it was going to be a rough night because some of them were already drunk. They were swigging down their beer and throwing their heads back, laughing. They were a rough and ready bunch. I ran back to the others and told the acts we were in trouble because the audience was more rabble than an audience. We all decided on a plan of attack. I told the comic who would be on first to keep his material pretty clean, because if we kept it clean, the audience might come around to our way of thinking.

'No problem,' he said, 'I'll get them round to our way of thinking.'

The huge Australian came in and asked if we were ready. We told him we were and that the comic was going on first. The show started and the comic went on. I couldn't believe my ears, he must have known every dirty joke in the book, not only was he swearing like a trooper, but he started to incite the audience and so, they started to get rowdier and rowdier. Meanwhile backstage I could see Ramona was getting very nervous. My heart went out to the poor girl. I knew that singing classical songs to a bunch of Australian miners who had been whipped up into frenzy was going to be so hard for her. She was going to 'die a death'. I made my way over to her and told her not to worry and if she got a hard time from them, she should just do one song and come off, we would cover for her, I added. She just looked at me disdainfully and arrogantly said, 'I'll be fine'.

Well, I was only trying to help. I walked away disgusted. In my heart I hoped that she would, 'die the death' and maybe she'd be brought down a peg or two. The comic finished and then he introduced her. I couldn't wait to see this, so I went and sat at the side of the stage. She went on with all the confidence in the world and began to sing 'I feel pretty' from the musical, *West Side Story*. The men went quiet for a moment and then they began to boo and cat-call her. I cringed and watched as she didn't seem bothered at all; she just carried on smiling and singing her song. Then, to my complete astonishment, she began to unbutton her dress. This lady who had been so high and mighty on the plane was a singing stripper. I couldn't believe my eyes. This woman who had treated us like scum on the plane was now undressing in front of a load of beer-swilling miners. I wondered what happened to her classical training. She finally stripped off every stitch of clothing and the crowd was going wild. I thought that must be the end of it, but no! I was wrong. She carried on singing and walked off the stage and into the midst of them. They started to paw her and do all sorts of things but she carried on smiling and singing as though nothing were happening. This woman had some nerve. Towards the end of the song she walked back on stage, finished the song and took a regal bow, as though she had just finished singing an aria from *Tosca*. I was so shocked. I couldn't believe what I had just witnessed. I rushed backstage to join the others, who were waiting to see what type of attitude she would have now. It was unbelievable. She just glided past us as though we didn't exist.

Because she was a stripper, I forgot my experience on the plane and thought I would try again, so I lied through my teeth and told her I liked her act. She just gave me a look that would have made the Sahara desert freeze over. I just lowered my eyes and walked away. But somewhere today in Australia lives a stripper who sings the greatest, 'I feel pretty' you have ever heard. How sad that she felt that she had to do that for money. I won't ever be able to understand it.

The next thing I heard was our name being announced. Now it was my turn to be nervous because I knew that Tommy and I had never been able to do dirty material. It just never felt right. Tonight was to be no exception. We went on expecting to be booed off but surprisingly the crowd seemed to warm to us. If it was because they had been satisfied with what had gone on before us, I will never know, but we started to do okay. We were getting laughs in the right places and we came off feeling really good. The night finished and all the acts, except Ramona, ended up at the bar. We started to crack jokes and discussed how we thought the night had gone. By this time in my life I had really begun to enjoy alcohol, it made me feel different, more confident and before the night was over I was well and truly drunk.

The following night came and we went to the club. The same miners who the previous night had been pawing and screaming over a stripper were tonight bringing their wives to see the show. I wonder if they had told them about their behaviour with the stripper. I guess not. Men tend to be cowards when it comes to that sort of thing. I was looking forward to this night, because I have never liked stag shows even though Tommy and I had done lots of them in the past. For some reason they always left me feeling dirty and unclean. So with it being a mixed audience tonight, it was going to feel much more comfortable without having to worry if we were being dirty enough or not.

Boy was I in for a surprise! All the acts went on, even the stripper, who just sang that night. Then came our turn and we were announced. We bounded on stage like an express train, ready to show the other acts just what Cannon and Ball were made of. We started the opening routine and we must have been on stage for about ten minutes and we hadn't even got a laugh yet, I mean not even a titter. The audience just glared at us as though we were from another planet. We could see the contempt in their eyes and feel the animosity towards us. Inside I began to crumble, my shirt was wet through with sweat, and my top lip and had begun to stick to my teeth (a sure sign of panic). I looked at Tommy, and I could see that he was resenting what the audience was doing to us. Suddenly from the back of the room someone started a slow handclap. It spread like wildfire and before long everyone in the club was joining in. On top of this they began to shout, 'Off, off!' It was the most terrible feeling I have ever had. I stopped the act and looked at Tommy. He was glaring back at the audience with hate in his eyes.

'Let's get off,' I said quietly.

Tommy looked at me for a moment and then said, 'No Bobby.'

I couldn't believe what he was saying, here we stood in front of an audience who hated us and there was Tommy saying that he was staying on.

He turned back to the audience and shouted, 'So you don't like the act then, eh!'

This incited the audience even further and they began to go berserk, shouting abuse and jeering. Now I could tell that Tommy was angry because he was now sneering back at them. I just stood there wishing the ground would open up and kindly take me away. We stood there for a few moments allowing all this abuse to hit us, every bit of which was like an arrow going through us.

Then Tommy shouted to the audience,

'You won't beat us,' then he turned to me and said, 'I had a dream last night.'

As soon as he had said that I looked at him as though he had gone crazy. He had started the first line of a routine that lasted ten minutes. And I knew that if he gave me a feed line I would have to give an answer back. I just stood there astonished. He just smiled and gave the feed line again.

'I had a dream last night,' he said.

I knew he would stand there all night waiting for my line back if he had to, so I decided to give him the line back to get it over with. We stood there for the next ten minutes doing a routine that no-one was listening to, they were too busy jeering and shouting abuse at us. Halfway through the routine Tommy and I began to laugh and we ended the routine nearly on the floor. We had become oblivious to them by now. At the end of the routine Tommy looked at the audience.

'Thank you ladies and gentlemen, for being such a 'different' audience, I hope we never meet again.'

Tommy then put his arm around my shoulder and we took a bow as though we had taken them by storm. What the audience hadn't realized was that by now we were taking the Mickey out of them. We left the stage and when we got back to the dressing-room the other acts were too embarrassed to talk to us. But that didn't bother us. We just went to the bar on our own and got drunk.

The next day we went back to Sydney and caught the plane to England. On the flight I knew I had to get back to reality, by that I meant Yvonne and the kids. It wasn't going to be easy. For the past six weeks I had enjoyed being single again. I knew that I had sent Yvonne hardly any money, so by now I was wondering how she had managed. It was funny how I had never thought of that in Australia. She had moved into our new house on her own, with no furniture of carpets, so I realized, without much remorse, that she must have had it rough.

When we arrived at Manchester airport, Yvonne, Joanne and our Mavis were waiting for me. It was so good to see them. Yvonne looked beautiful. I hugged and kissed her and then scooped my daughter up into my arms and held her close. I didn't realize until that moment just how much I had missed them. I said my goodbyes to Tommy and set off for my new home. During the ride I told Yvonne not to worry about furniture and things, that we would get them in the time ahead; she just looked at me and smiled. She then told me that she had had to go into debt for some new clothes so that she would look nice for when I came home. I felt guilty and told her it was okay, she could have anything she wanted. We arrived at the street that led onto Harewood Road and when we turned the corner I couldn't believe my eyes. There were banners draped right across the road saying, 'Welcome Home Bobby'. All the neighbours were at their front doors cheering me.

Now this was very strange for me because I didn't know any of them, it was the first time I had been to the house. What I hadn't realized was that Yvonne had already lived there for six weeks and by now knew every one of them. Even though I didn't know them it was a wonderful gesture. We arrived outside our and I got out of the car, I waved to the neighbours and we went inside. What greeted my eyes was something I will never forget for the rest of my life. Yvonne stood to one side and let me go in first. I expected to see an empty house, but to my surprise it was fully furnished. It looked beautiful. It had a settee, armchairs, carpets and even a television. It looked terrific, but I knew we were in trouble because we didn't have the money to pay for all these things. I looked at Yvonne and asked her how much debt we were in. She smiled and said none. I couldn't believe her. I sat her down, took hold of her hands and explained that she didn't have to be afraid to tell me. She told me that with her family allowance and the money I had sent her, she had scrimped and saved, even to the extent that she and Joanne had lived on baked beans on toast. So we didn't have any debt whatsoever. Everything was fully paid for. I broke down crying. I had never felt so guilty in my entire life. Here was the woman that I had married, scrimping and saving to give me a nice home, and there I had been in Australia, womanizing and drinking and just thinking of myself. I loved that woman and at that moment I felt that I was too big a rat to be in the same room as her. She took hold of me and loved me as a mother would love a baby. I promised I would make it up to her, but it would take me another fifteen years to do that. Looking back now I see that I was on a downward slope that only Jesus could save me from. I wish that I could have opened my heart up to Him then, but I was too caught up loving myself to even have any room for Jesus.

I quickly settled into my new house and loved it. It felt good to know that at last I had given Yvonne a house that she could call her own. The neighbours were a lovely bunch of people who went out of their way to make us feel welcome and before long we were all popping into one another's houses without even knocking.

From the time we moved into Harewood Road, our career seemed to move into top gear. Before long we were topping the bills in the big nightclubs and were getting a reputation in show business as a good act. One day our manager phoned to tell us he had got us a spot on a popular television program which was running at that time called *The Wheeltappers' and Shunters' Social Club*. The show was the brainchild of a man named Johnny Hamp. He was a lovely fellow who loved variety. He brought us another popular show named 'The Comedians', and many other shows of that nature. Sadly, he no longer works in the television business, and there a very few men like him around in TV anymore, and that is such a handicap for today's T.V. The show was made in the studio and the set was made to resemble a working men's club, hence the title. The set was so realistic that the viewers thought it was a real club and they would write in and ask if they could become members.

The show was hosted by Bernard Manning and Colin Crompton, two comedians I admire for their wonderful comic timing and ability to work an audience. Bernard was the host and Colin played the concert chairman, complete with flat cap. Bernard is still working as a stand up comedian but sadly Colin is no longer with us. He looked as though he had been washed up on a beach and was a great comic. They had each learned their craft in the nightclubs, going great in one place and dying in the next. They both knew how to please different audiences and it was a pleasure to watch them work. It's a shame that the new comics who are coming through have nowhere to hone their talents as the cabaret clubs mostly died out long ago.

Tommy and I learned a lot from Bernard and Colin. They had been around a long time and were worth listening to. Bernard had a cabaret club in Manchester and Tommy and I had worked there before we became comics, Bernard used to give us advice. He has a bigger heart than anyone gives him credit for and does a lot of work for charity which goes unnoticed. A lot of people don't understand Bernard Manning, they think he is controversial and he has a problem with some people, but he is like that with everybody and no-one can escape his acid-tongue and quick fire wit.

Anyway the night came to do the show and we went down to the studio. It had been years since we had been in a TV studio, (Opportunity Knocks) and Tommy and I felt strange having to do the act in front of cameras. We were very nervous and Bernard could see it, so he tool us to one side and told us to forget the cameras and just work the act as if we were in his club. We took his advice and went on and stormed the audience. We were even asked to come back again.

Meanwhile, back on the home front, Yvonne had taken control of the money and was paying all the bills and giving me spending money. I know this doesn't sound right, but it was my idea as it always burned a hole in my pocket. One day I got fed up of this situation and told Yvonne that as I was the man of the house, I should take control of all the money and pay all the bills. (I can hear the feminists screaming now, but sorry ladies, I am what I am.) Yvonne agreed, having first making me promise that I would, in fact, pay all the bills. She did not want to go back to all the bad times, she said, when all that we were paying were debts. I told her not to worry, I wasn't a child anymore and I knew what my priorities were. I took control of the money and, about a week later, I was walking through Shaw when I noticed a tumble drier in a shop window. I knew that Yvonne had always wanted one, so I decided to buy it for her. I went into the shop and told the man that I wanted the tumble drier in the window. He asked me if I wanted it on hire purchase. I told him no, I would be paying in cash, and asked if he could tie a big blue ribbon around it. He looked at me as though I had gone mad. I mean, who puts a big blue ribbon around a tumble drier? But he did as I had asked and before long I was heading home with a tumble drier which had a great big blue ribbon around it. When I arrived home I told Yvonne to go upstairs and not to come down until I shouted. She asked what was wrong and I told her that everything was fine; it was just that I had a surprise for her. She went upstairs and I got out the tumble drier and set it right in the middle of the lounge. I then shouted Yvonne to come down and waited for her reaction. She walked in and let out a scream. She was so excited. I was almost as excited as she was, it was great to see her happy. She then seemed to ask me a hundred questions in one breath.

Where did I get it from?

How did I manage to get it home?

What made me buy it?

Eventually she calmed down and just sat there looking at it. After a while she asked me the million dollar
question.

How did I manage to pay for it?

I shifted a little in my seat and told her not to worry,
she was adamant, where had the money come from to
pay for it? I explained that I had decided to leave the
bills this week and would pay double next week. I saw a
shadow of anxiety cross her eyes. She had let me take
control and I had blown it. She sat me down and
explained to me that we wouldn't have double the
money next week to pay the bills. I knew then in my
heart that I had let her down once more. I tried to explain
that I had only wanted to see her happy, and that it
wouldn't happen again. She just smiled at me and said
she understood. That was the day I realized that money
for me was a weakness. From that day on Yvonne has
always taken care of our finances.

For two reasons 1976 was a very important year for
me. One of them was because we got an offer to do a
pantomime at the Bradford Alhambra. And the second
was that it was during this pantomime that I met a man
who would play a very crucial part in my life. We had
been offered the role of the broker's men in the production of *Jack and the Beanstalk,* starring Charlie Drake and
Jack Smethurst. Tommy and I were very excited about
doing the pantomime because we had never done one
before and it meant that we would be working in a real
theatre at last. When we got the scripts we realized that
we would be the fourth comics on the bill, (which means
that we would be the last to get any laughs as the other
comics would get all the laughs before us.) It didn't
bother us too much, as we reasoned it was a great chance

to learn the ropes. When we read the scripts we didn't understand some of the jargon, like 'enter O.P.' or 'exit U.S.' or 'Stand C.S.' because Tommy and I had never had to go from a script before and we didn't know what these things meant we decided to ignore them, thinking they probably weren't for us or something. We soon found out that they were for us, much to our embarrassment. On the first day of rehearsals we met Charlie Drake, a comic with a touch of genius. I have never seen anybody who could make the audience laugh hysterically one minute and have them crying the next. And then we met Jack Smethurst, who was a very popular actor of the day.

With Tommy and me being so far down the bill, we were more or less looked upon as part of the chorus. It didn't bother us, as I said before, we were doing a real theatre at last, we had to wear make-up and read scripts. It was brilliant. After we had met with everyone we began to rehearse the show. We had memorized our lines well but it was the other secret signs that we didn't know. We kept coming on in the wrong place, bumping into people as we were going off, standing in the wrong place when we were on stage. We could see the director rolling his eyes and getting impatient with us. After about half an hour he couldn't have been able to take any more and called a halt to the rehearsal. He took us both to one side and asked us if we knew what O.P., U.S., and C.S., meant in our script. We lowered our eyes and told him sheepishly that we didn't have a clue. He told us what these secret abbreviations were, if it said in the script 'stand C.S.', it meant 'stand centre stage' (simple isn't it?); if it said 'exit U.S.', it meant 'get off up stage', and 'enter O.P.' meant 'come on opposite prompt side' which was the opposite side to wherever the stage manager was situated. (I know that must have bored you, but everybody needs to a place where they can turn the light off and go to sleep!)

The panto opened and we went down very well. Every

night when I wasn't on stage, I would be in the wings (the side of the stage) watching Charlie Drake. I studied him. It was unbelievable how the audience would go wild as he walked on stage, and he would just stand there for a few moments wallowing in all the attention. I wanted what he had, I wanted to be loved by an audience the way he was. I thought that would satisfy me and fill the empty feeling deep in my soul that I had for quite a while. I learned so much just from watching him.

After about two weeks into the pantomime, I began to find the nightlife in Bradford. I started to go to the discos and I was having a great time. It was one long party and I was boozing about four nights a week and loving every minute of it. I had got a taste for whisky and coke and this, coupled with the ladies, was a great ego booster.

One day a man walked into my dressing room and introduced himself. He told me his name was Max Wigley. He explained that he was the theatre Chaplain. I shook hands with him, thinking to myself that I was in for a very boring time for the next ten minutes. I had met 'God people' before, and they always seemed to be holier-than-thou do-gooders. I was wrong about Max. He was different from any religious person I had ever met before. He was only a young man, but he was genuine and had a peace about him that I just couldn't understand. His face always seemed to be laughing, and his eyes cared. He was interested in what I had to say and, that first time, he never mentioned God once. We got on well and chatted for a while about how the show was going and then we said our goodbyes. As he was leaving, he asked if it would be okay if he popped in again. I liked him and told him it would be fine and he left. I didn't realize that that had been my first step on the road to meeting the Lord.

A week or so passed when there was a knock on the door. I shouted, 'Come in,' and in walked Max. The devil must have been on my shoulder because I wasn't glad to

147

see him. Again I thought I was going to have a boring, tedious few minutes. He sat down and asked how things were going and made small talk for a few minutes. Then he asked me a question which made me sit up and think. He said,

'Are you happy?'

I told him that I was very happy and he just smiled. I hadn't realized the depth of that question, but he did. It hit me hard. For some reason I thought he was attacking me with a question like that and went immediately on the defensive. It's hard to be faced with the truth and the devil certainly doesn't like it either. So because I had thought he'd attacked me with that question I retaliated by firing questions back at him. Thinking back, he hadn't even mentioned Jesus once. It was I who started to ask all the questions, then again; maybe Max knew that I would. I asked why he wore a 'dog' collar. Did it make him think he was better than me? Max laughed and replied that he didn't particularly like wearing it, but it was a rule of the church, and Vicars had to wear them. He explained that what he wore had nothing to do with loving God, and as far as thinking he was better than me, he said it was his aim to serve me. He was beginning to blow my mind away. The way he talked about God as though he was his best friend. Now, all my life I had believed in God, like many other people, I knew that when I died I wanted to be on the right side. I was sure that as I was pretty kind-hearted and hadn't done anybody any wrong God would look at me and I would be alright, and here was a man who was telling me that I was all wrong. I tried to explain to him that I hadn't done anything particularly bad and that I had been kind to some people along the way, I told him that when I was in any kind of trouble I prayed too. He just sat there listening to me making excuses for myself and it was beginning to unnerve me. So I asked him what made him so sure that he would end up in heaven. What he told me took quite a while to sink in, twelve years in fact. He told me that he had asked the Lord to forgive him for being a sinner, and that the Lord had entered his life. I didn't fully understand what he meant by this, because at that stage in my life, I didn't see myself as a sinner. I didn't know that I had been born into sin. We talked for about half an hour, discussing the Lord and various things, and then I made my excuses and went on stage.

A few days later he called again. I was beginning to feel that I would never get away from him. We talked for a while and he said he had brought me some books to read. I felt guilty that I was feeling so resentful towards him. When we had finished chatting he asked what we were doing after the show. I told him that I was going out to the disco and was ready for a good night out. Suddenly he asked if it would be possible if he could come along with us. I almost laughed out loud.

'No!' I told him, 'I'm not going out with someone wearing a dog collar, and besides, you might stop me from pulling the women if they see I'm with a vicar.'

He just laughed at me,

'No problem,' he said and pulled off his collar, 'See! I'm just like you now.'

This made me laugh so I invited him along. We had a great night and he became a wonderful friend. At the end of the pantomime run we said farewell to one another and went our separate ways, he with his God, and me with my career. It was to be over twelve years before I would be the one who was frantically knocking on Max's door, and on that occasion he would lead me to find God for myself.

Chapter 6

The Fame Years

Moving on a couple of years me and Tommy were now topping the bill in small clubs and had worked our way up in theatre to second top. The first time we topped the bill in a nightclub was at the Fiesta Club in Sheffield. We had been there many a time as a support act and this particular week we had been booked to appear as a support act for Matt Munro. As the week began on the Sunday we turned up as we usually did for band call in the afternoon. When we arrived we were told by the manager that Matt Munro had cancelled because he was not feeling well. The manager liked Tommy and me so he told us he was going to put us at the top of the bill. We couldn't believe what he was saying. This was a big nightclub which seated about twelve hundred people and he was giving us the chance to top the bill. We felt a bit nervous and excited, this was unbelievable! The manager could see by our faces that we didn't believe him so he walked us outside where the billboard with the stars names, in lights, were situated. We watched, awestruck, as a man pulled down Matt Munro's name and put ours up. It was a wonderful feeling, to see our name up in lights,

'*Starring all week, Cannon and Ball!*'

We went back into the club and the manager took us to the stars' dressing room. Tommy and I were amazed. It had a shower, settees and a bar filled with every drink you could imagine. The beauty of it was that the star didn't have to pay for what he drank. So, as the manager said, 'we were stars'. I felt a million dollars.

We settled in and waited for the first night to arrive and arrive it did. We went around all the other dressing rooms saying our 'hello's' to the all of the 'support acts' and becoming generally big-headed when one of the supports pointed out that we were in for a rough night. We didn't understand and asked why he would say such a thing the others all agreed that the audience had booked to see Matt Munro and that they wouldn't be getting what they had paid to see. This brought us right back down to earth as we could see that they were right. We now felt under pressure and went back to our dressing-room in a panic. What if they didn't like us? What if they booed us off? What if they all walked out? Tommy and I talked about all these things and the more we talked, the more nervous we became.

Before we knew where we were it was 'top of the bill' time. Us! The compare explained to the audience that Matt Munro had been unable to make it and then introduced us. We went on and the place was packed. Five minutes into our act we had them eating out of our hands. We had a fantastic night. We couldn't have gone down any better. We came off and the manager was waiting in the wings ready to shake our hands. He told us that we had no problems; we could top the bill all week. We stayed on at the club, basking in our glory. I was in no hurry to rush home to Yvonne, this was far more exciting.

The following night we went to the club, ready to slay them again but when we arrived there, the manager was waiting for us. I could see that something was wrong by the look on his face. He told us that the club owners had been in touch with him and they had got Freddie Starr to top the bill for the rest of the week. He apologized, saying that we were still on the bill and then he dropped the bombshell. With Freddie Starr and ourselves both being comedians, we would have to go on before the girl singer so that we didn't clash. Not only had we been dropped from the top of the bill, now we were at the bottom! The manager kept apologizing, but nothing he could say would lift the rejection we were feeling. We looked up and saw that our names were already down and Freddie's name was in our place. We made our way sadly to the star's dressing room and emptied it of our clothes. We looked around at the free booze and shower and made our way to the little support's dressing room down the corridor.

After we had been on I stayed around to watch Freddie. I could see why he was the top of the bill. He was and still is a comic genius. I watched him and realized that I had a long way to go to be anywhere near as good as he was. Even today I am a fan. I think he is the most underrated comic this country has. By the time the week had ended, Freddie and I had become good friends and even today I still count him as a friend.

Time went on and we started to earn good money so Yvonne and I didn't have to worry too much. We even decided to move house to a better we had spotted which overlooked a golf course. We put ours up for sale and before long we had sold it and moved into our new house. It was an old pre-war semi-detached with lots of steps leading up to the front door, it was a lovely old house with lots of character. The only drawback was the golf course. The first tee was right at the back of my garden and I can tell you if there is one thing I don't like are people who look down their nose at others, and some of the golfers could be so snobbish and rude. Allow me to explain! One day I was playing with Joanne outside in the garden and she was running around squealing and giggling. Suddenly a man who was on the first tee shouted to me in a voice which sounded as though he were chewing marbles (falsely posh!),

'Excuse me,' He shouted, clearly angry, 'would you mind keeping that child quiet, I am trying to tee off!'

I looked at him and all I could see was a pompous old man. I could feel my temper rising.

'No, I will not keep the child quiet,' I shouted back, 'And another thing, this is private property and if my daughter wants to scream and shout it is her prerogative to do so!'

He looked back at me, obviously shocked that someone would dare to talk to him like that, but I had him on the run and I wasn't about to let go.

'And another thing you can think about,' I continued, 'is for you to be quiet in future when you are teeing off, because if I hear you shout "FORE!" I will report you for disturbing the peace!'

He seemed to shrink and quickly hit his ball and was off. And from that day forward, the golf club and I never saw eye to eye.

I remember quite vividly the start of my fame years, my adulation years, my money years, whatever you wish to call them. I call them my shallow years, because ever since I became a Christian, I realize now that no matter what anyone attains to in this world, it is shallow without God

In 1978, Tommy and I were doing a club called the Heart of the Midlands in Nottingham and our Manager, Laurie Mansfield, (by this time we had two managers, one in the north and Laurie in London) sent a man named Peter Woodley from his office to see us in the Midlands club with a producer from London Weekend Television. Peter Woodley was one hundred per cent behind Tommy and me. He used to come to lots of our gigs and tell us that it was his life's goal to get us to the top. We believed him, and it felt good to have somebody who believed in us so strongly. He had previously brought everybody and anybody from television to see us, but they had always knocked him back saying that we weren't right for television. But Laurie Mansfield, Stuart Littlewood and Peter had faith in us, so at least there were three people rooting for us.

Peter phoned us in the afternoon and told us that the producer was making excuses not to come, but he would try his best to get him there. So by the time it reached ten-thirty that night we just knew they weren't able to make it. We went on stage and paralyzed them. The crowd went crazy, they were up on there feet, shouting, 'Encore, encore'. We took four bows that night. We came off and wished that the man from London Weekend Television had been there to see it. We were just discussing this when the door opened and in walked Peter Woodley with the television producer. Peter told us that they had made it just in time to see our show. He introduced us to the producer. His name was Humphrey Barclay and he said that he'd enjoyed the show. He was a nice man and seemed very interested in our act. He fired lots of questions at us and left, saying that we would meet again. Peter told us later that on the train back to London he had spent half the time trying to sell us to Humphrey and all the time Humphrey was saying he liked us. But Peter kept on selling us like a good agent would. Eventually Humphrey stopped him mid-sentence and said,

"Peter, will you stop trying to sell the act. I have been trying to tell you for the last half and hour that I like them."

Peter then realized that he was so used to people putting us down that when someone said they liked us he couldn't believe it. We heard nothing for a while until Laurie Mansfield called us and told us that London Weekend Television were putting out a program called *Bruce's Big Night Out*, hosted by Bruce Forsyth. He went on to say that the program would last three hours and would consist of lots of different things. Humphrey Barclay, who had seen us in Nottingham, wanted us to do six five-minute segments to fit within the show. We were over the moon. At last, a chance to make it big.

That summer we were booked to appear in summer season with Larry Grayson, famous for his camp catch-phrase, 'Shut that door'. We were there for twelve weeks and during this time the television company wanted us to record the segments down in London. This created a host of problems for us as we had already signed the contracts for the season. Knowing that it was too good an opportunity to miss we asked the promoter who had put on the season if we could have some Fridays off to record the show, thankfully he said yes. It was going to be a long slog for Tommy and me, because it meant that every day for six weeks we would have to travel to London to rehearse and then back to Great Yarmouth for the show at night.

We met the writer, David McKellen, and instantly got on with him. He had written for us six five-minute sketches which were very funny, but neither Tommy nor I had ever done a sketch before. They needed acting out and we had never acted before either, we were just two comics. Nevertheless, we memorized our lines and hoped for the best.

Summer arrived and we made our way up to Great Yarmouth. It was great, we settled into the house we had rented for the summer and then went out on the town to enjoy ourselves before the hard work began. The show soon got underway and Tommy and I were going down well with the audiences. Then the day arrived for us to go to London to rehearse the sketches. The night before, Tommy had suggested that we went to bed early because we had to catch the train at six o'clock the following morning. How could I sleep? There was no way I could go to bed early as the adrenalin from being on stage still pumped around my body for quite some time after I had been on. It always took a while for me to come down and relax afterward. So Tommy, wisely, went to bed and I went off to the nightclub. I must have had a lot to drink because no sooner had my head hit the pillow than it seemed I was on the train to London seeking fame and fortune. I can still feel my head bouncing off the train window as I kept dropping off to sleep.

When we arrived in the capital we headed for the rehearsal room. Once there we met the man who would be directing us, Geoff Sax. He was lovely and helped us tremendously in those early days. He seemed to sense that Tommy and I were out of our depth and went out of his way to make us feel comfortable. We rehearsed the first day and soon got into the swing of things. Before long it was four o'clock and time to catch our train back to Great Yarmouth to do the show. We caught the train and were full of excitement and expectations for the future, and arrived back with just enough time left to get to the theatre before we were on. We did this every day for six weeks; up each morning to catch the six o'clock train to London, rehearse the sketch and then back on the train to Great Yarmouth for the show.

Friday was the night that we recorded the show, but during the day we had to do a camera rehearsal. This was very tiring because all day we just went over and over the same sketch so that the cameras knew exactly where the moves were and so on and so on. During the afternoon of the first recording, Humphrey came into the studio and called me to one side. He asked me why I parted my hair down the centre. I told him that I had always done that because it made me look funny. He looked at me for a moment and then gave me some sound advice. He told me that I was naturally funny and what I was doing was called 'gilding the lily'. I didn't understand what he meant, and didn't want to look stupid so I nodded my head. He could see that I didn't understand so he went into more detail. He told me that to be truly funny comes from inside of a comic and not his appearance. Now I understood. All these years I had been parting my hair down the middle so that people would think, 'Ah, here comes the funny one,' instead of people finding out for themselves. I thanked him and un-parted my hair. I could have been a very different Bobby Ball if he hadn't given me that advice. We went on in the evening and recorded the sketch and did very well considering Tommy and I had never acted before.

After about two week of this heavy schedule, I was becoming fed up with being up early, the train journey and then straight to bed after the show. I told Tommy that this was no fun for me. I wasn't having a proper drink, not to mention all the women I was missing. He told me that I would have to hang in there because this was a chance of a lifetime and we couldn't afford to mess it up just because I wanted to enjoy myself. I agreed, but I wasn't going to listen to him. That night, after the show ended Tommy and I said our goodbyes, he headed for his bed and I headed for the nearest disco. I boogied nearly all night, getting back to the rented house for about four o'clock in the morning, feeling the worse for the booze. I set my alarm clock for five-thirty and fell on the bed in a drunken stupor. Suddenly my eyes shot open and I knew something was wrong, I looked at the alarm clock and it said six o'clock. I had overslept. Not only that, I was still wearing the clothes that I had on the night before. I quickly changed my clothes and raced to the station like I was on fire. When I arrived Tommy was waiting, tapping his foot and trying to control his temper. He wasn't at all happy and informed me, through clenched teeth, that we had missed the train. The next one was at eight o'clock, and to make matters worse, it wasn't an express train. I felt very guilty and apologized repeatedly. I was feeling like a naughty schoolboy. He calmed down and said we should catch the eight o'clock train and take our chances. Eventually the train came and we got on. Tommy wasn't speaking to me. Mind you, he didn't have the chance because I kept on apologizing the whole way there. We got a cab when we arrived in London and told the driver to hurry as we were now four hours late. When we reached the rehearsal room there was nobody there. It was empty! On the table in the centre of the room was a note. Tommy picked it up and read it out. It said that they had got sick of waiting and had gone back to the studios; we had broken our contract so they had no alternative but to terminate it.

Tommy and I looked at each other. We both felt the same, sick to our stomach. At that precise moment words could not express accurately just how I felt. It was all my fault. I had ruined everything for us both. If it hadn't been for me wanting to have a drink and showing off in front of women, we would have caught the train and everything would be fine. I looked at Tommy and once again apologized, this time it was from the heart. He just looked at me and told me not to worry; we would just have to try again. Then, suddenly, from behind tables and out of doors jumped the whole team, Geoff Sax and everyone! They were laughing their heads off. They had set us up and they had played a blinder! We were so relieved, and tried to explain why we were late but they wouldn't listen, they just kept on going on about how they'd wound us up. Tommy and I looked at each other and knew that we had got through this one by the skin of our teeth. Anybody else apart from Geoff Sax would have sacked us. With a sense of relief, and having learned a valuable lesson, we gratefully spent what little time we had rehearsing.

From then on we got down to serious business and spent the rest of the season rehearsing and recording the shows. It had been such a punishing schedule and we were drained. When we finished, we sat back to wait for them to be shown. They showed the first program but it was a disaster. I thought Bruce was brilliant but the format was all wrong. An even bigger disappointment was that we were not on it. We phone Laurie Mansfield in London and he told us that the show was too long and the big bosses at London Weekend had decided to scrap the segments which we had recorded. We were devastated. All that work for nothing. It wasn't as though we had been paid a fortune for it either, we got £400 a show. He told us not to worry too much; at least we were still working. It didn't help the way we felt though.

It's funny but sometimes acts think that managers don't do anything besides sit back in their offices and draw money, (don't get me wrong, there are many who are sharks and are just in this business to rip people off), but there are a precious few who work hard for their acts. This type of manager doesn't tell the act what they are doing for them, in case they are disappointed if it doesn't come off. That's what happened with Laurie Mansfield. When he told us not to worry, we thought that he didn't care, but later found out that he did. He marched right over to London Weekend Television to see one of the top men there at that time, the great David Bell. David Bell is now no longer with us, but he is very sadly missed. He loved variety and was responsible for a lot of the good television that we saw in the early eighties.

Laurie told David that he wasn't happy with them not showing Cannon and Ball, after all the work we had put in and that he wanted to see the man at the very top to complain. David said he would arrange an appointment for him and he go along too, as he was a fan of our. The next day Laurie and David went along to see Michael Grade, the man who ran LWT, a very powerful man in television. He asked Laurie and David into his office and invited them to sit down. Laurie refused, he said he'd prefer to stand and demanded to know from Mr. Grade why he wasn't showing us. Mr. Grade told Laurie that it was nothing to do with us personally, it was just that the idea of a three-hour show wasn't working, he'd had to cut a lot of things out and we happened to be one of the casualties. Laurie told him that he didn't think it was fair as we were human beings and not a product. He then went on to tell him just how hard we had worked, traveling from Great Yarmouth to London every day and the whole saga. Mr. Grade said he understood and felt sorry for us, but their was nothing he could do, he had a television station to run. Laurie asked him if he had seen any of the stuff we had recorded and Mr. Grade said that he hadn't so Laurie asked if he would take a look at it. The man at the top replied he would watch it at his first convenient moment and Laurie and David left the office.

Laurie Mansfield didn't tell us any of this, and I only found out what had happened when I began to research this book. Mr. Grade was true to his word, because that same night he watched what we had recorded. The next morning he telephoned Laurie at his office and told him that London Weekend Television were prepared to give us out own series. This was brilliant news! At last we were going to be stars. It was also the road which would eventually lead me to God.

After all that, it all seemed to happen rather quickly. One minute we were bottom of the bill and now agents were phoning our managers wanting us to be top. We were told that we had to go to London for a few days, first to meet David Bell and secondly to meet the writer who would be writing our series. We arrived in London with instructions to meet David Bell at two thirty at the Ritz hotel for afternoon tea! Even to think about it was unbelievable; there were Tommy and I, two red-nosed comics from council estates in Oldham, meeting one of the most important men in show-business at none other than the Ritz, for *afternoon tea*!

I had never been to a business meeting before, so I asked Yvonne if I should go dressed up or casual. She told me to go as myself. That I should go dressed how I would feel comfortable. There was no need for her to tell me twice, I put on my jeans and a tee-shirt, with my old duffel coat which by now was a second skin to me, and set off for the Ritz.

When Tommy and I arrived at the Hotel, the maitre d' stared at me, horrified. I don't think he had ever had anyone arrive at his establishment in jeans and a tee-shirt before. He swiftly took me to one side and explained that he couldn't allow anyone in without a tie. Luckily David Bell spotted us in trouble and explained to the Maitre d' that we were guests of his. The man spluttered and coughed and tried to show his authority before finally backing down, saying that he would find me a tie from somewhere. I felt like a second-class citizen, all because I had no tie. After I had put my borrowed tie on (which looked even more silly on my bare neck with a t-shirt), we sat down in the lounge and made light conversation while David called the man over and ordered tea and sandwiches. After the maitre d' had gone we began to discuss the series. Before long, he was back, asking me to take off my duffel coat. I said yes and handed it to him. The look on his face was a picture. I thought he was going to have a heart attack. He told me that 'sir' would have to wear a jacket. It's funny, isn't it, how someone can call you sir yet look at you as though you have leprosy. Well he did. Not only was he making me feel stupid and insignificant, but I felt that he was taking away all credibility I had with David Bell. I glared at the maitre d' and informed him that it was impossible for to wear a jacket when I didn't have one with me. He then told 'sir' not to worry, he would get me one. He whisked away my treasured old duffel coat and came back with a jacket, which I subserviently put on.

I was now feeling very embarrassed as this had all gone on in the presence of London's finest. I was sitting in the middle of all this affluence in a borrowed Jacket and tie, in a tee-shirt and I felt about as welcome as a flea. I must have looked like a mime artist. I glanced sheepishly at Mr. Bell and wished the ground would open up and take me out of there, but he found the whole thing very amusing. He understood the ridiculousness of it all. Before long we were all laughing and I knew that David was one of us, a genuine person who laughed at all the pomp and hypocrisy. Suddenly, the 'sir' person was back with our tea and sandwiches, and it took all of our strength to keep ourselves from laughing. After we had our meeting we prepared to leave and David said he would get the bill. I gave my borrowed clothes back as David was paying the bill. I just couldn't believe the price, it was £40. It was incomprehensible to me how a few sandwiches and tea could cost so much, when it costs about £1 or so for a packet of tea bags and not much less for a loaf of bread. How they get away with prices like that, I'll never know, but maybe it's just to keep the 'riff-raff' out!

Our meeting the next day was with the writer. David had told us that they had commissioned a man called Sid Green to write the series. He told us we had to meet him at LWT's restaurant. Tommy and I were looking forward to meeting Mr. Green, because to us he was a comedy legend. He had written most of Morecambe and Wise's material and now he was going to write for us. We walked into the restaurant and saw him seated at a table eating his lunch. David, Tommy and I walked over to where he was and sat down. David introduced us and we said our hello's. He just looked at us and then went back to his food. We thought we had done something wrong. I glanced at David who was sitting with a mischievous smile on his lips. He was interested to see what would happen when three big egos's got together.

After an embarrassing silence of about two minutes, which seemed like hours, Sid looked up and stared

directly at me. He slowly put down his cutlery and said,
'Well, to tell the truth, my wife doesn't like you.'

Tommy and I were dumbfounded; this was a statement we most definitely weren't expecting.

'I've watched those things you recorded,' he carried
on, still looking at me, 'and you have a lot to learn.'

Tommy and I couldn't answer, it was as if we had lost
our tongues.

'And another thing,' he said, 'those silly braces and
those stupid Hush Puppies will have to go.'

Now he had said the wrong thing. It was one thing to
tell us that his wife didn't like us and that we had a lot to
learn, that was fine, but to tell me that my braces and
Hush Puppies would have to go; he was most definitely
overstepping the mark. I didn't care who he was, I
wasn't going to have a man sit there and tell me that the
character I had worked on for the last fifteen years was
going to change overnight. I looked at him and he had
gone back to eating his meal. I was getting angry.

'Excuse me, Mr. Green,' I said.

'Yes,' he replied, looking up.

'My braces, and my Hush Puppies will be staying,' I
said, 'and another thing,' I continued, 'as for your wife
not liking us, my wife has never liked Morecambe and
Wise, particularly when you were writing for them.'

I was lying, of course, my wife liked Morecambe and
Wise as much as I did, but by this time I had had enough
of being looked down on. He again put his knife and
fork down and looked at me. The thought crossed my
mind that I had just ruined our chance of working with
one of the best writers in the business, but I'd had to say
it. His stony face slowly started to break into a grin and
then he laughed.

'I think we can work together,' he said.

He had just wanted to see how I would react and obviously I reacted in the right way because Sid not only
wrote our first series, but many more after that. It was his

material which helped to make us famous, and we learnt such a lot from him.

We went back home and then a few moths after, returned to London to record the series. It was a whole new experience for Tommy and me. LWT had booked us into the Savoy Hotel and we had limousines to take us everywhere. We were living like stars. It was all absolutely mind-blowing. We recorded all the episodes in the series and Tommy and I thought they had gone well. Sid was pleased and to me that mattered more than anything else. At this stage we were relatively unknown but that would soon change. When the series was due out, all the press had got behind us and they built us up and declared that we were going to be stars. Everything was ready for our big day and we were looking forward to it with anticipation. Then came the bombshell. Four days before the first show, the technicians at LWT went on strike. Our series wasn't going to be shown. It was pandemonium. Laurie Mansfield and David Bell had 'panic' meetings, Laurie Mansfield needed the show to be shown, otherwise all the plans he had made for the future would be jeopardized. The press started to call us Cannon and Blackout, which I thought was funny, but no-one else, got the joke. It was a horrendous time for Laurie, because if the strike went on longer than the time allowed for our slot, then we wouldn't get shown until the following year. Thankfully for us the strike was called off just in time and our first series got shown. The response was something beyond our wildest dreams. Suddenly, after years of obscurity, everybody seemed to know us, and it was amazing. Everywhere we went people would be shouting out our names, in the streets, the pubs, even taxi-drivers in the centre of London would stop their cabs and shout, 'Hello Bobby, hello Tommy'. And everyone had begun to shout 'Rock on Tommy' wherever we were. It was as if they knew us personally. It was something that we were not at all used to, but we liked it very much, it made us feel like we were accepted. When we were halfway through our series, London Weekend Television offered us a three-year contract at a fee never paid to anybody before. Our future was looking secure, but Tommy and I didn't think about that, we were too caught up in the adulation that we were receiving.

The first season we did as top of the bill, after our first T.V series, was in 1980. We were booked to do fifteen weeks, two shows a night at the North Pier Theatre, Blackpool. It was quite a daunting thought as we hadn't ever topped the bill in a theatre before. But we had no need to worry. We went to rehearsals and met the other acts on the bill. At the bottom of the bill was a young comic who I knew would be a star the very moment I saw him. I told him so too. He was a young lad with a vitality that was hard to match and he had talent too. But at that stage in his life it was raw. He would go on stage and work like a whirlwind for ten minutes and come off leaving the audience screaming for more. His name was Lenny Henry, and even then he was hit by racist jokes which sometimes hurt him even though he pretended they didn't. I feel pleased to see that my prediction came true and Lenny has now become one of Britain's brightest stars, married to a very funny lady by the name of Dawn French.

During the first week of rehearsals for our show in Blackpool, as Tommy and I were walking to the theatre we turned a corner which led to the street facing the pier, and what we saw made us stop dead in our tracks. They had just put up the posters advertising the show, and there it was, a huge poster, about thirty feet long, with out names emblazoned across it, 'The Cannon and Ball Show.' It was a marvelous feeling. At last there we were topping the bill at one of the best theatres in the country. And this time there would be no pulling our names down, as though it had been by accident. Suddenly a bus went past with our faces spread along the side of it. At last, we had arrived.

Tommy and I went on to the theatre, walking on air. We took the same route the next day, just to have a look at the posters again, but this time we were in for a shock. As we turned the corner, there was a queue of people lining up to buy advance tickets to see us. The amazing thing was that the ticket queue was about three quarters of a mile long. It started from the ticket box at the North Pier and went all the way along the seafront right up to Central Pier. It was a wonderful sight. These people were queuing to see Tommy and me. This fed my ego big-time, making me think more of myself than Yvonne and the kids.

On opening night we walked on stage and couldn't speak for about ten minutes for the crowd cheering and clapping us. I didn't even have to try and be funny, all I had to do was look at Tommy and the audience would fall about. Dotted about among the audience I could see people dressed up as me, complete with braces, curly wigs and moustaches, shouting 'Rock on Tommy!' Many people have asked me where my catchphrase of 'Rock on Tommy! Came from, well just before we made it big, a friend of mine by the name of David Essex, recorded a song called 'Rock on'. One night during the act Tommy began to sing and I started to say 'Rock on Tommy,' it stuck and before long people started to laugh at it. Don't ask me why, but they did. And on that opening night in Blackpool all the audience were shouting, 'Rock on Tommy.' And so it has stuck with us ever since. You see, a good catchphrase can't be written, it just happens naturally. That year we broke the theatre box office record at the North Pier since it opened. And it's been open for at least one hundred years. Our success as comedians was unprecedented, it was as though we were pop stars, no other comedian had had this kind of success and we were mobbed everywhere we went. I know it sounds big-headed, but it is the truth, the audience would even rush the stage at the end of the show, it was a lot to handle and we loved it. But I am only telling you this so you may understand why I eventually realized that I need the Lord's forgiveness.

Quite a funny thing happened that season that I don't think has happened very often. We were packing them in every night, and Lord Delfont, who owned the theatre decided to take a trip up to Blackpool to find out what all the fuss was about. He came all the way up the pier only to be told that even he couldn't get in as every single seat had been sold. It really tickled his sense of humour that here he was, the owner of the theatre, and he was being refused admission. But he was very gracious about it and came back the following night and really enjoyed himself. All over Blackpool people were selling red braces with 'Rock on Tommy' printed on them, and it was amazing to see that suddenly young people began to wear them, not just red braces, but braces of every colour. Suddenly in the early eighties braces became fashionable again. We decided to open our own souvenir stall and it was strange to see pens and cups and all sorts of things with our names and pictures on them. I was like a tourist myself because I even had a mug with my own picture on to drink from, (how's that for egotism?).

That year, Blackpool asked us if we would be prepared to switch on the famous illuminations. This is an annual thing in Blackpool, they spend thousands of pounds on the bright lights and visitors come from all over the place to see them. For anyone who comes from the north of England, as Tommy and I do, it is one of the biggest honours of their career to be asked to switch on the lights. Tommy and I of course said we would, and when I told my mother that we were switching on the lights, she flashed a huge grin and said, 'Now you really are a star!' We told the committee who organized the switching on of the lights that we had a problem as we were working that night on the pier and we had two shows to do. They worked it out and said that we could switch on the lights in between shows. They knew it would be impossible for us to walk down the pier in time so they organized a car to come down to the end of the pier, to the theatre and pick us complete with a police escort. This was the first time a car had been on the pier since it opened so once again we were honoured.

On the night of the switch-on we finished the first show and waited for the car to pick us up. It came in due course and we got in. It was an amazing experience because we had to run through a line of policemen to get into the car. The pier was lined six deep either side of the car with people, they were lined up all the way down the pier. It was frightening. I understand now how a rock star or royalty must feel like when they are mobbed with people and paparazzi. And we were not rock stars or royalty, just two little comics from Oldham.

The people were pushing and shoving, trying to get at us, they were in a frenzy. I did a silly thing and opened the window a little to get some air and before I knew it someone had thrust their hand inside and was trying to rip out a chunk of my hair. It was horrific. The car slowly made its way through the throng, down the pier and when we arrived at the square where we had to turn the lights on, forty thousand people were waiting for us. It's no wonder our heads got turned. We began to think that we could do no wrong, everything was happening too fast. We climbed up onto the podium to switch on the illuminations. All the people cheered their approval and on the podium with us we had a big golden cannon filled with Blackpool rock which was to blast out at the time of the switch on. After a countdown we pulled the switch and Blackpool lit up and me along with it.

As my mother had said, now I really was a star. All the dreams I had cherished during the early days of working the clubs with Tommy had now come true and had far surpassed what I could have ever imagined. I felt that I was standing on top of Blackpool Tower itself. The only trouble was, that while my career had reached its peak, my personal life was about to plunge in the opposite direction.

Chapter 7

Freefall

Now I was a star my life changed rapidly. Doors began to open for me wherever I went. No longer did I have to wait and see if I could get into a disco, I was given star treatment. I would simply get someone to phone up a disco and tell them I was coming and they would set a table aside for me and my friends. Then when I arrived they would surround us with bodyguards. It wasn't long before I was thinking that this was all natural. I began to drink whisky very heavily and after a while everything you say and do is being controlled by the alcohol that is running around your brain. I also started to notice that it was quite easy for me to attract women. I thought it was because of my overwhelming good looks and personality, my pride would let me see that it was nothing to do with either of those, it was because I was on television and it made those women feel good to be seen with a celebrity. In reality, I was their conquest, not the other way around. The truth of the matter is that I am five foot four, with hair like a toilet brush, gappy teeth and more wrinkles than a map of the London Underground. Only a woman like my Yvonne could love someone like me. And to tell you the truth I'm glad she does.

So with the drinking and the women, I was well and

truly on my way down. As my career skyrocketed, my personal life had taken a kamikaze dive towards a crash. Along with women and drinking, I found that I was becoming angry at the slightest thing. If I went out to a disco or had a little too much to drink, I had a desire to fight. It wasn't that I hated those people who I picked fights with; it was simply pent up aggression. I enjoyed the atmosphere of it all. It was very easy for me to pick fights because I always had bodyguards surrounding me, not like the poor person I'd decided to pick on. He would have no-one. So really, he'd be a much more courageous person than I. Nevertheless, this was how my life was changing.

Yvonne and the kids were beginning to take a place further to the back of my mind as I searched for a greater enjoyment. Don't get me wrong, I loved them and would never hurt them, or so I thought, but more and more I was beginning to think about myself.

I finished the summer season in Blackpool with more enemies than friends. The reason I say that is because I didn't suffer fools gladly. If something was wrong I would throw a tantrum because, a) I liked everything to be perfect, and b) I thought that's what stars did. There was no-one to tell me to stop behaving like a prima donna and act like a normal, decent human being. As Yvonne says, 'a lot of us don't know we are doing wrong until God shows us.'

After the season had ended Tommy and I went down to London to record the Christmas Special. It was during my time there that I went really wild. I must have hit every club in London. By this time, the management had got us a personal assistant, a man by the name of Trevor Davies. His job was to drive us around and literally do anything that we required him to do. Now my egotistical world really opened. I ordered him around like a servant. Ordered him to do all sorts of things, bring me this; bring me that. He had a terrible job, and if he reads this book, I would like him to get in touch with me so that I can apologize for the way I treated him.

Stringfellows Nightclub became my favourite haunt when I was in London. It was a disco then and not the club it is now. But as I was drunk most of the time, my memory of what I did there has become a blur; this is probably a good thing. One night I do remember vividly, however, has stayed with me for all the wrong reasons. I'd been drinking quite heavily and me and some lads had decided to finish the night off at Stringfellows. Yvonne had just bought me a fashionable (then) full length raincoat which reached down to my ankles, when I wore it I thought I looked so fabulous. When you entered Stringfellows there was a restaurant then a bar and then facing you was the stairs which take you down to the disco.

'Come on lads, lets go down to the disco,' I shouted loudly so that everyone could hear me. The lads started to follow me as I made my way over to the stairs. By this time the whole club was watching me as I had made enough noise to wake the dead. I got to the top of the stairs, when suddenly, to my horror, my heel got caught in the hem of my raincoat. Down I went, head over heels down the stairs. I landed spread-eagled on my back at the bottom. I could hear all the people in the club laughing at me, and as I looked up, I could see all my friends looking down at me. They just laughed and then they left me. I should have felt embarrassed, but I didn't. I simply dusted myself off and marched into the disco as if nothing had happened. To tell you the truth, I felt as though I had just made a great entrance.

Yvonne and I were now making quite a lot of money so we decided to move house again. We lived next door but one to the local school and by now there was a constant knocking on our front door. We needed a place which was more out of the way. I told her that I hadn't got time to go house-hunting and she was to go and find one that she liked. Yvonne never complained about anything she just accepted my behaviour and carried on quietly. I went on with my show-business life while Yvonne and our Mavis went house hunting. It wasn't long before Yvonne said she had seen a house and asked if I would go along with her to see it. I agreed and we went to see this house that was high up on a hill. It was a beautiful old cottage with a breathtaking view and even though it was more rural, it was only a two-minute drive from my parents' and our Mavis. We said we would have it and after all the paperwork was completed, we moved in. It's funny, but the house was named, 'Halfway House' and looking back that was exactly where I was in my life.

Now I felt that I had kept my promise to Yvonne. That night all those years ago, when we were in the back bedroom of our Mavis's, and I had promised her a big house and a big car to go with it. I had got her the big house, now all I had to do was to get the big car. That Christmas Tommy and I were appearing in Coventry in a Christmas Special. We had sold out for the entire run and everything was looking good. A few months earlier, I had bought the car of my dreams, a little white, Corvette Stingray. Yvonne was very unhappy with it as it was hardly what you would call a family car. It had two seats and a tiny space in the back where Joanne had to be squashed into. I knew Yvonne was right, but I loved my Stingray, it was an animal. Anyway one day Tommy and I decided to play a game we loved to play. We would put on our oldest, scruffiest clothes and then go around shopping in all the upper class shops and see how the salesmen would react. This day we went around the upper class car showrooms. It was funny but the higher up in the car market you went, the more snobbish the salesmen became, and then when they realized who we were, they would immediately change and run around trying to do everything they could to get us to buy one of their cars. More often than not, Tommy and I would just walk out, pretending to be mightily offended and when we got outside we'd laugh like naughty schoolchildren at what we just did.

This particular day Tommy and I had decided to go to the Mercedes dealership to play our game, on the way there we passed a garage which had three gold Rolls Royce's in the window. We changed our mind, this was the place. We went in and to our surprise the salesmen, who didn't recognize us, still treated us like human beings. Tommy and I were impressed by this. After about half an hour, Tommy had fallen in love with one of the cars. Then he got a crazy idea that we should have a Rolls Royce each.

'Come on Bobby,' he said, using his best persuasive technique, 'Let's get one each. We deserve it after all those years of struggling.'

Apart from my dreams in our Mavis's back bedroom, I have never been the least bit interested in getting a Rolls Royce, they just never appealed to me, I like fast cars, sports cars, or big American cars, but slowly, Tommy was talking me into it. After a while I gave in. The salesman agreed to take my beloved Stingray in part-exchange. It broke my heart to see him drive it away. I said if he could get all the paperwork together for the weekend, I'd collect the car then. In the meantime I phoned Yvonne and told her that I had got rid of the Stingray and bought another car. She asked me what I had bought so I decided to wind her up. I told her that I'd bought an MG, but she didn't know what that was, so I told her it was another little sports car, with wire wheels and a lovely red colour.

I don't think I've ever heard Yvonne shout like she did then. She told me that I was a selfish person and that I wasn't being fair to Joanne, because this would mean that we couldn't ever go out as a family. I knew how she was feeling, but I wasn't going to back down from my joke. I told her that I would be home at the weekend and then she could see it for herself. I told her that it was the car that I'd dreamed of all my life. We ended the conversation and she told me sarcastically that as long as I was happy that was all that mattered. I wanted to give in and tell her I was only joking, but I decided to carry on with my plot.

The weekend came and the salesman delivered my Rolls Royce to the theatre. It was shiny gold with a private number plate, JR 17. I didn't know what it meant but it felt good to me. After the show I set off for home in my new car. I find it hard to describe the feeling of driving a Rolls Royce. Some people love them and some people hate them. Me? I just didn't feel as you should when you buy a new car, even a Rolls Royce. I just felt that an ordinary working class person like me didn't belong in one. Don't ask me why, it's just how I felt. Anyway, I put all these feelings to the back of my mind and made my way home. When I arrived, it was quite late at night and I put the car in the garage as quietly as I could and went through to the lounge where Yvonne was waiting for me.

'It's in the garage, Yvonne,' I said, trying not to laugh.

If looks could kill then I should have died then. She looked at me as if I'd committed murder.

'I don't want to look at it,' she said, 'I still think you are one of the most selfish people I have ever known.'

I begged and cajoled her and eventually she gave in. We walked through the kitchen to the garage and I let her go first. When she saw the Rolls Royce, she let out a scream.

'Where did you get the money from?' she screeched. I told her not to worry, as it was, in fact second hand. Later the press wrote that Tommy and I had bought two brand new matching gold Rolls Royce's, but in reality they were second hand and cost £17,000 each, roughly the price of a new family saloon car. She calmed down and said that she was happy it was anything other than a new sports car.

The next day we went off to show my mother and father, to make them really proud of their son. As we drove there, I looked at Yvonne and could tell that she wasn't enjoying the drive at all. I asked her what was the matter, and she told me that she didn't like it. She said it made her feel like a snob. She had put into words exactly how I was feeling. A Rolls Royce is a great car, but that day I found it wasn't for me. As we were on our way to my mothers I could see people stopping to look and they looked at us with contempt, and I felt that I had let them down. The Rolls Royce had separated me from the ordinary man that I thought I was. I arrived at my parents' house and led them outside to see the car.

'Do you like it?' I asked them, hoping they would be proud of me.

'It's a big 'un, isn't it?' exclaimed my mother.

'It'll be heavy on petrol, that will,' my father quickly followed up.

I realized that they didn't even know what it was, and they were speaking the truth in ignorance.

'Do you know what kind of car it is?' I asked.

They just looked at it and shook their heads. I could see that they didn't have a clue.

'It's a Rolls Royce!' I declared, trying to whip up some enthusiasm.

'Well, it's nice,' replied my mother, trying to please me.

'Aye, you've done well lad,' my father said, understanding that it was some kind of status symbol.

I knew that my parents were simple folk. I realized then that they didn't have time for fancy cars and all the material things the world had to offer. They were happy with their lot, and as long as their children were alright they were happy.

'Well' I thought to myself, 'at least I've got the big car that I promised Yvonne.'

It didn't last long. We had it for about two months and then I got rid of it. I bought another sports car instead, but at least this one had two little back seats. One thing that I did find out from that escapade was that Yvonne also wanted a simple life. It was I who wanted all the trappings of success. Now I realize that no riches on earth can mach the richness of knowing God. Only His grace can bring you closer to Him.

My father had always said, 'There are no pockets in shrouds.'

Around 1982-3 we were booked into the Dominion Theatre in the West End of London. We were booked for six weeks at two shows a night, and it was the first time we had worked in the West End, and we were quite nervous how the tickets would sell. The box office at the theatre phoned our management about two weeks before we were due to open and informed them that we had sold out for the full six weeks. It was marvelous news, not only were we going to have full houses but we had sold out even before we had arrived. Apparently they were now selling tickets on the black market for £50. This news only sent my pride into overdrive.

By this time, I had a personal assistant of my own. I had offered Trevor, our Mavis's husband the job and he had accepted. I had known Trev since we were kids so it felt good to have a mate with me. We arrived in London and started to paint the town red. At first Trevor was a bit lost as to what to do in the job, but eventually he turned out to be one of the best P.A.'s in the business. He would lift me up when I got down, and was always there for me, no matter what mood I was in. I wasn't in London long, before I discovered Speaker's Corner at Hyde Park. I would go down there on a Sunday afternoon. It found it fascinating and before long I had joined in with the hecklers who would go out of their way to shout at the religious speakers. There I was trying to shout down these men who were speaking about the

Lord, but whatever I said, it never threw them, they had conviction. Perhaps it was this that I didn't understand. Some of them would stand there, full of the Holy Spirit, praising God and I would shout out to them. But I would always leave with more thoughts about God than I had when I had arrived.

It was during my visits to Speaker's Corner that I became friendly with a tramp by the name of Smithy. I never knew his real name; he just preferred to be known as 'Smithy' so I adhered to his wishes. He was an old man who would tramp around the streets of London and make his way to Speakers Corner for the Sunday debates. He chose to live this way and was full of life; I can still see him now, wearing his long overcoat that had seen better days and tatty old trousers. He had shoes with holes in them and being a tramp, he didn't take too many baths, so you had to be careful not to get downwind of him. But the one thing I will never forget was his eyes, they were alive, they sparkled like diamonds and he was always laughing. Whatever had happened in his life to send him to those depths, I will never know, but he was such a character and his sense of humour was still intact. One particular Saturday night during our run at the Dominion, I looked up at the boxes at the side of the theatre, usually reserved for royalty. In them were some celebrities who had come to see Tommy and me. This put a thought into my mind. For some reason I thought that those boxes were associated with privileged people so I decided to do something about that. The next day I went to Speakers Corner and told Smithy I had booked him a box at one of our shows and invited him along as my guest. He got very excited and I could see he was as pleased as punch. The night that he was coming I arranged for Trev to meet him outside and then escort him to his box. About half an hour later Trev came into the dressing room and said that he had bought Smithy some champagne and chocolates and he was now happy sitting in his box, feeling like royalty. The news about this tramp in the box spread like wildfire among the cast. Every time any of the cast went on stage they would keep casting their eyes in the direction of Smithy's box. Inside I was having a secret chuckle to myself because I could imagine Smithy feeling like a king for the night, looking down on people instead of people looking down on him. Tommy and I went on stage at the end of the show and introduced him. Everyone's eyes in the theatre looked up towards Smithy's box. They didn't know who he was, but as he was sitting the royal box they presumed he was an eccentric celebrity, so they started to applaud, and true to form, Smithy stood up and did the most flamboyant bow I have ever seen anybody do. I don't know what the audience thought of him, but I didn't care. If the box was good enough for celebrities it was good enough for anybody. I will never forget Smithy, because he really was one of God's children, he just didn't know it.

My visits to speaker's corner started to have an effect on me. I started to find that whenever I came away after laughing at and heckling the religious speakers I felt I had been doing wrong. It also left me with a restless feeling and discontentment in my heart. I had every material thing that the world could give me, but yet I had this empty feeling. Stardom or whatever we want to call it just didn't fulfill me anymore.

I started to listen what the speakers were saying instead of heckling them, and found that I was getting interested. What they were saying began to make sense to me. I bought myself a bible and tried to understand it but it was useless. What the speakers had said made sense, but reading the bible was like learning a foreign language. Nevertheless I carried on, trying somehow to find the truth that the speakers were talking about. But it was no good, because I was trying to find the truth with my head and not with my heart. I started to talk to

Buddhist's, Jehovah's Witnesses, even Mormons, anybody who could lead me to the truth. I read their literature in an attempt to find some answers. But every one of their religions left me empty. There was no-one who could tell me what I really wanted to know. There were always rules involved. As far as the Lord was concerned I asked God all the usual questions; how can God allow all the suffering? How was the human race started if Adam and Eve had only three children? (Or so I thought). How do we know that there really was a Jesus? What I didn't realize was that I had to come to Jesus first before I could understand fully. In the meantime I would have to continue on my way until I could no longer turn my face away from Jesus.

In the early eighties, I met Max Wigley, the theatre chaplain, again and began to ask him more serious questions about God. Slowly our friendship developed and we became good friends. Whenever I was in Bradford, Max would come and see me and I would always turn the conversations back to God. So looking back on it, the Lord was already drawing me, even at that time in my life.

In the four years from 1982 to 1986, it was crazy. Tommy and I were working non-stop and always away from home doing summer seasons, tours, T.V and panto. We were continually on the road, so it became a very lonely existence, but I could always find myself a whisky and a woman to help me through it. The routine was always the same; we would get into town, check into the hotel, go to the theatre, do the show, hit a disco till the early hours of the morning, get drunk, maybe have a fight and then back to the hotel and roll into bed. Then the following morning we would get up, travel to the next town and the same routine would begin again. There were no nights off. There were many 'downers' on the road, sadness was always there, waiting, but we did have quite a few laughs too.

I remember Oxford with fond memories. Trev and I had been out to a disco which finished about three o'clock in the morning and we decided to go back to the hotel. We had parked the car in a municipal car park at the other side of town, so Trev suggested that we got a taxi back to the hotel and pick the car up in the morning. But with the alcohol inside me, I was having none of this. Trev tried to make me see sense but to no avail. We eventually arrived at the car park and picked the car up. As we came down the ramp, the barrier was down, I told Trevor to put some money in the machine. He just looked at me and said it was no use. I argued that he was talking stupid because all he had to do was put money in the thing and the barrier would go up. He didn't answer but just pointed to the sign on the wall which read; 'this garage is not twenty-four hour parking.' We started to laugh, but I wasn't going to be beaten. I told him that if I could lift the barrier high enough, perhaps he could get the car underneath. By now I had a Camaro sports car and it was quite low to the ground. Trev agreed so I got out of the car to try and lift the barrier. It started to move. My plan was going swimmingly, when suddenly it broke and left me holding half of it in my hands. I looked at Trev and we both started to laugh. We laughed so much; we were going weak at the knees. Then suddenly our laughter was cut short. A police car pulled up in front of us. A young policeman got out and looked at me as if I was one of the great train robbers. I sobered up in a minute.

'What's going on?' He asked

I thought that was a stupid question as it was obvious, but I decided against voicing my opinions. I thought I'd better explain, and then he would see that I was an innocent man.

'It's like this, officer,' I began, trying to be as jolly as I could, 'we came and tried to get our car out of the car park, but we couldn't because the barrier was down, so I tried to lift the barrier, but I didn't break it.'

'Well', he looked at me smugly; 'you're holding it' I looked down to see that I was still holding half a barrier. I started to stammer and plead my case, but he wasn't listening.

'Come on,' he said, 'I'm taking you both down to the station.'

'What for?' I said, I was horrified, 'It was an accident.'

'Vandalism,' he replied.

I knew then that he was just after me, and nothing I said was going to change his mind. We arrived at the police station and stood in front of the desk.

'Stand behind the white line,' said the young policeman. He was very official. Just then an old sergeant turned up and quickly weighed up the situation. He looked at me and winked. The young policeman whispered a few words to him and then asked Trevor to step forward. Before he had a chance, I stepped forward myself and pleaded with the old sergeant, trying to tell him that it was all a big mistake.

'Get behind the line!' The young policeman snapped.

He was beginning to get on my nerves.

'I have sons as old as him,' I thought to myself, but nonetheless I did as I was told. Trevor stepped forward and the young man asked him to empty his pockets. This really frightened me, because Trevor was carrying about £4000, which was used to pay for hotels and things during the tour. I saw the policeman's eyes light up and I began to worry that they might think we had stolen it. I knew I had to explain where it had come from and what it was for, so I stepped forward again,

'You don't understand,' I began,

'Get behind the line!' the young policeman shouted again. This time I wasn't listening to him. I was talking to the old sergeant,

'You see, we always carry that sort of money when we are on tour,' I continued, trying to get Trev and myself off the hook.

'Get behind the line!' the young policeman shouted again.

'No!' I said, 'because you're not listening to me.' I was pleading with him now,

'Take him down to the cells,' the young policeman said to another policeman standing by. I looked at Trevor, he leaned towards me,

'Tell 'em nothing,' he said, as the policeman got hold of my arm.

I couldn't believe what was happening to me. I was being taken down to the cells for trying to explain and Trev had started to act like a major villain. As I was taken away, I could hear Trevor shouting after me,

'Tell 'em nothing.'

This was crazy, all over a car park barrier that I was willing to pay for. By the time I had reached the cells, my attitude had changed. I was beginning to feel like Clint Eastwood in the film, *Alcatraz.*

'Can you remove your shoelaces, please?' the policeman asked me.

He was a nice man, who knew what had happened was a mistake, but it wasn't his call, and so he had to follow orders. I wasn't bothered how nice he was, by this time, I had joined in the gangster game.

'What do you think I'm gonna do, commit suicide?' I retorted, almost feeling my lip curl.

He just smiled, and continued being patient with me.

'Would you like a blanket?' he asked.

Was he being funny, how dare he insult me. I had now become harder than Clint Eastwood. I was now Sylvester Stallone.

'No, I'll be fine.' I replied

I walked into the cell and he locked the door behind me. I looked around the room and at the little peep-hole in the door, and felt terribly alone. I had never in my life been in a cell before and it wasn't a nice feeling. After about ten minutes my gangster mode had left me feeling foolish and I sat on the bench, shivering. It was freezing in there. It was no use; I would have to call the nice policeman back. Swallowing my pride I banged on the door. There was no reaction to my banging, so I carried on. After a short while the door opened and the nice policeman was standing there with a smile on his face, and holding a blanket.

'Do you want a blanket now?' He said, as if he didn't know.

'Is it possible?' I said in my most submissive voice.

'Course it is,' he replied and handed it to me. I said thanks and went back to sit on my bench. He stood there looking at me for a moment, and I could see that he was beginning to feel sorry for me.

'Would you like a cup of coffee?' he asked.

Would I? I could have kissed him. He brought me a coffee, and after about ten minutes they came to collect me. At least I was getting out of the cells. They took me to an empty interview room and told me to sit down. The door was open and across the corridor from me, I could see Trevor arguing with a policeman. Suddenly he spotted me and shouted what had now become his catch-phrase,

'Tell 'em nothing.'

I turned my eyes away, not wanting to get involved. I sat there for a few minutes before the young policeman who had arrested us came in. He sat facing me with a load of papers. He began to ask me questions. I answered them truthfully and kept telling him that it was all a mistake, but he was having none of it, he was determined to get me for vandalism. We were getting nowhere when the old sergeant came in. He whispered something in the young policeman's ear, and they both walked out. After a while the young policeman came back looking rather sheepish. He told me that they were going to forget it this time and let me off with a caution, but I would have to pay for the barrier. I knew that the old sergeant had spoken to him and must have told him that he was pushing it too far. I agreed to pay for the barrier and then they said I could go.

When I got to the front desk, Trevor was there waiting for me. I smiled at him and then turned around to the young policeman who had arrested us and asked him if he was married. He replied that he was, so I invited him and his wife to the show the following night. He was overjoyed and said it would be great. I shook hands with them all and said that I'd see the young man at the theatre. When we got outside, Trev looked at me and remarked that I must be crazy asking 'that copper' to the show. But Trev didn't know what I had in mind. I told him to make sure that two seats were available in the front row for my 'new found friend'.

The next night came and Tommy and I went on stage. I saw the policeman there with his wife. This was my territory now and my time for revenge had come. His joy soon turned to embarrassment when I began to rib him. I do it all the time, but this night was different, I didn't just do it playfully for a minute or two, but for a t least fifteen minutes. I cracked every gag I could about him and I think that if there had been a hole in the floor, he would have crawled into it. We came off and I knew he wouldn't be coming backstage to see me, so I sent Trevor to try and find him, but he had gone.

During this time, money was no object to Tommy and me. It was top hotels with limousines here and there, and if we had to travel any further than five-hundred miles, there would be a chartered plane to take us there. I had begun to believe this lifestyle I was living. If we were due to go to a theatre, we would check out what the dressing rooms were like and if they weren't up to scratch, we would have them refurbished, even though we would only be using them for one season. Extravagance became our middle name.

Once, we had been booked to do a private show in

Brighton and at the time I was staying in a suite in a posh hotel in London, so we ordered two limousines. We booked two suites costing £350 each at a plush Brighton hotel and went down there, used the two suites as changing rooms, did the show and then went back to London. In all we must have used those suites for all of a quarter of an hour. What waste! The Lord must have been looking down on me and shaking His head.

The pressure on Tommy and me at this time was intense. Underneath all this extravagance we were two ordinary lads who got caught up in all we were receiving. Sure we had chased fame, and found it, but sometimes that kind of adulation went too far. It had changed me dramatically. I was boozing more than ever, and lust had well and truly got its hold on me, not to mention the aggression. Yvonne had got used to me flying of the handle, so to her it was an everyday thing. She began to think that that was the way I was. One day, feeling guilty about my attitude, I decided to change my ways and be more positive. I told everyone that I had found the 'quality of life', that I'd no longer be losing my temper because it just wasn't worth it. I went around declaring, 'the quality of life.' It became a bit of a catch-phrase. Trevor just rolled his eyes, Yvonne shook her head and our company manager and friend, a man named Tony Hayes, just smiled.

Shortly after I had made my statement about the quality of life, we were traveling up to Birmingham from London. We were in the middle of a tour and on one of those rare occasions when I had decided to take Yvonne. In the car with us were Tony Hayes and his wife Anita and of course Trevor. We were driving along very nicely on the M1, when my car decided break down. Normally if anything like that happened, I would have gone berserk, but not this time, now I had the 'quality of life'. Everyone looked at me, waiting for me to blow a fuse and they were all quite surprised when nothing happened. Calmly, I told Trevor to get the AA and then I proceeded to get out of the car, take a table and two folding chairs from the boot and put them on the hard shoulder. Everyone in the car was looking at me as though I had gone mad. I then took out a chess set and put it on the table and set it up. It was all extremely civilized and I asked if anyone was interested in a game. I can still see their faces. They just looked at me with their mouths hanging open. It must have been a sight to see, a man at a table on the hard shoulder of the M1, waiting for someone to play him at chess. Eventually Tony said he would play and he sat opposite me. They still couldn't get over my 'quality of life'. We had been playing for about five minutes, when a huge lorry flew past and blew the table and all the chess pieces onto the grass verge. I jumped up and started to scream every swear word I could think of. 'Quality of life' had gone out of the window. I started to shout after the lorry, but by now it was miles away. I turned around and glared at the others, they were all trying hard not to laugh. This just made it worse for me. I turned my back on them, got on my hands and knees, trying to find all the chess pieces and all the time muttering under my breath. While I was doing this, Yvonne walked over to me and tapped me on the shoulder. I looked up at her and she said,

'So much for the quality of life, eh?'

She was right; my quality of life had lasted all of two days.

It was during this time, that I found myself having a couple of days at home. But I couldn't stay in with my wife. I always had to be out and about showing myself off. The couple of days that I had off landed on a weekend, so I decided to go for a drink on the Sunday lunch time with a couple of friends at a local wine bar called 'Nell Racker's'. I know it's a strange name, but it was supposedly named after a local ghost. Anyway we arrived at the place and got settled in at the end of the bar. On the one side of me stood a huge man who looked as though he could have killed the heavyweight boxer, Mike Tyson. He started to look at me so I looked back at him and after we had looked each other up and down we began to talk and he told me that I had taken the Mickey out of him a few years previously at a club in Manchester. I tried to smile but my lips were stuck to my teeth, I didn't know whether he was going to hit me or laugh about it. We carried on talking and found that we had much in common and, both of us were fans of rock 'n' roll. The more I talked to him, the more I liked him, he was a real character and we got on very well. After a while, I went to the gents and when I got in there a man asked me if I knew who I was talking to. I said I didn't, so he informed me that he was named Jack Thirsk. He was known as a local hard man and had a very dubious past. He warned me to be very careful what I said as Jack would take my head off, without thinking about it. This perturbed me a little because a) I had been getting on famously with him and b) I had become very fond of my head. I went back to my place at the bar and he was still there. We carried on talking and I found him to be a very interesting man. He introduced himself properly and said that he had enjoyed my company. We said our goodbyes and agreed to meet again, which we did. Jack and I became close friends and together bought the club where we first met. We named it Braces.

As I said before, by now money was no object and I would spend my money on anything that took my fancy. Looking back I am amazed at the type of person I had become. The devil had really got a hold of me. One summer season in Scarborough, I fulfilled a lifelong dream and bought a little boat which I named *Smile*. It was a smashing little boat and we had some great times on it. The next year we were in Torquay and after seeing the boats there, it wasn't good enough for me. I wanted something bigger and flashy, something everyone would look at. One morning, I saw a big forty foot boat come into the harbour, and I knew I had to have it. It had a 'For Sale' sign on the side, so all I had to do was talk Yvonne into having it. I told Yvonne I had seen a boat that I'd fallen in love with and that I would like to have it. She reasoned with me that we were only in Torquay for ten weeks and after that the boat would be no good to us. I promised her that I would keep the boat forever and that I would never want or ask for another thing. She gave in to my pleading eyes and phoned the people who owned the boat, telling them that we would be coming down to discuss the details with them. We arrived at the dock and when I saw the boat, I fell even more in love with it. It was a Tremlett boat with a captain's bridge and all the gadgets that anyone could think of. I could see that it didn't interest Yvonne in the slightest and that she was only doing this for me.

Now I have never been any good at bargaining so I left it to Yvonne, who is quite good at it. She asked the people the price they were asking for the boat, and they told her £40,000. Both Yvonne and I knew that this was way out of our price range, but I had to have this boat at all costs. Yvonne tried to bargain with them, but I wouldn't let her, I just jumped in and said I had to have it, at any price. Yvonne just looked at me, she knew there was no way that she could bargain now. She calmed me down and said we'd think it over and be in contact with them and then we left. When we got off the boat, Yvonne told me in no uncertain terms that there was no way we could afford to spend £40,000 on a boat. It was crazy, she said. I told her that I had to have it, it was something I'd always wanted and it would be a dream come true if I could have it. She gave in to me once again. And the next day we bought the boat. It was so big that I had a hard time handling it. It weighed fifteen tones so you can imagine it wasn't easy.

One Saturday night, a few weeks after I'd bought the boat, I decided that I was going to take it across the channel to Jersey for the weekend. I knew a man called Mac who told me he could take it across with me because he knew what to do. That was all I needed to know. I arranged to go the following Saturday after the show, during the night. I didn't tell Yvonne until the Friday before we were due to go, so that it would be too late to back out. After the show on Saturday, I had, as usual drunk my daily dose of alcohol. In fact I was rather tipsy, the excitement along with the alcohol meant that I felt more drunk than usual. It was a very foolish thing, trying to get across the English Channel, in the dark and drunk. But in those days, no-one could tell me anything. I knew it all. We all got in the boat and set off for Jersey. I was on the captain's bridge with this chap, Mack, who said he knew what he was doing and Yvonne was downstairs with the man's wife in the cabin and Joanne and her friend had gone to bed in their cabin. It was fine until we left the sight of land and then I began to sober up. I was suddenly overwhelmed by a feeling of loneliness. It was a strange feeling and it made me realize just how foolish I had been. But we were too far out now to turn back. I felt that we were the smallest thing in the world afloat on the biggest sea. All sorts of things went through my mind; what if we hit something and it tore a hole in the boat? What if we overturned, would I have enough strength to save Yvonne and Joanne? (Yvonne couldn't swim then). These thoughts and many more went through my mind as I steered the boat. At that time, the sea was calm, but that didn't stop me from worrying. All around us I could see lights from other ships, but I knew that if we went down, they wouldn't know about it.

Suddenly to the starboard side of me I saw a red light that I took to be the back end of a boat. It was fine because it had passed us by. So I carried on going straight. Suddenly all these lights went on in front of me and sirens started to sound. I wondered what on earth was happening. Then I saw from the lights that the other boat was a mile-long tanker, and I was heading right for the centre of it. I was within a hare's breath of crashing into it. It was looming over me like Goliath must have towered over David. I thought that my days were about to come to an end. I banged my boat into reverse and turned the wheel. Through God's mercy I found myself just missing the back of the tanker. But now we were caught up in the wake. We were thrown about like a piece of wood in the rapids. Things were flying about the inside of the boat. It was all over before we knew where we were, but it was very scary while it lasted. We were once again floating along on a calm sea. The man who had said he knew what to do *then* told me that the English Channel was one of the busiest waters in the world. I asked him which way we should head now. It was then that he dropped the bombshell. He said he didn't know, because he had never left the shoreline before. Thanks! We were now in the middle of the English Channel without a clue where we should go next. Luckily for him that I had sobered up otherwise I might have thrown him overboard. I knew that Jersey was south of England so I looked at my compass and set a course south. After about an hour, I could see a dark outline of land in the distance. I still didn't have a clue where we were so I suggested that we anchored and waited until light. We all agreed and Yvonne and I settled down to get some sleep. The time was now about four o'clock in the morning and it would soon be light, so at least we would be able to see what we were doing.

Yvonne and I had been in bed for about two minutes when the boat started to vibrate with a loud noise which was deafening. I jumped out of bed and dashed up to the deck. Right beside my boat was a trawler that had decided to fish there. I had an intense feeling of relief. At last we had somebody near us who knew what they were doing. I shouted to them and all the crew came to the side of the boat. I asked them where we were and they all started laughing. They had recognized me and this only made it worse. They started ribbing me, but I was too tired to answer back. After a bit of chit chat I asked them what was the piece of land that I could see in the distance? Dawn was breaking now so the land was even more visible. They told me it was Guernsey and that Jersey was 'just around the corner'. They could see that we were novices so they warned us that Jersey was very dangerous to approach because of rocks and we should phone the coastguard to take us in. We thanked them very much for all their help and set off for Jersey, phoning the coastguard on the way. They came and led us in and thankfully, we arrived safely.

We had a nice weekend in Jersey and met up with friends we had made from years earlier when Tommy and I had done a summer season there, and on Monday morning we said our goodbyes and set off, sober this time, back to Torquay. It was raining slightly when we left the harbour, but when we got out into the open sea we found ourselves in the middle of a force six gale. I have never seen waves so huge. They towered over the boat, threatening to swamp us at any minute. One minute we were on top of a wave, and the next we were down in the belly of it. It was very frightening. It never bothered Yvonne; she only thought I was going too fast. What I didn't know as I was fighting against this raging sea, was, that with the sea being so rough, it was throwing everything around in the cabin and Yvonne was blaming me for going too fast. I quickly realized that it was hopeless and far too dangerous for another attempt and radioed the coastguard again and they came and took us back into the safety of the harbour. I had a show to do that night and had to get back to Torquay so Yvonne and I flew back and left the boat in Jersey. Mack and his wife would bring the boat back when it was safer. It wasn't until a couple of days later that I realized just how reckless I had been with my family's lives. If it hadn't been for the grace of God we might not have made it and been here today. I kept the boat until the end of the season and then sold it at a loss. I had spent a considerable amount of money on ten weeks enjoyment, my priorities were so wrong.

It was during this time, between 1982 and 1986, I was so full of myself and everything I did was to excess. I had everything but inside began to find myself feeling empty. Nothing was enough to please me, or satisfy me. I was searching for something to make me feel right. It was okay at first, because I didn't notice it too much. I was too caught up in this fast paced life. Along with this life came guilt. Guilt at the way I had treated my wife over the years. I tried to put these feelings to the back of my mind by buying some big car or another expensive 'toy' I could get excited about, and it would work for a couple of days and then the feelings would resurface, gnawing at my conscience. Eventually these feelings tormented me constantly, but I couldn't stop what I was doing, it was a vicious circle. I needed help and it was a lot nearer than I thought.

Chapter 8

Journey into a New Life

When we first began to do well in 1980, a company, called Wigwam Acoustics, worked for Tommy and me. They are a sound company and did all the sound at our gigs. I gradually got to know a few of the guys and found out that some were Christians. Not only that, but they were those, 'Born-Again Christians'. I had read my Bible so I felt quite knowledgeable, but I didn't understand what a 'Born-Again Christian' was and having these Christians around gave me a chance to study them. I had never been this close to one before, apart from Max Wigley, but he was a vicar so in my mind it was his job, but these were ordinary lads in ordinary jobs. They seemed to have a peace that eluded me, but I thought that I had it right, not them. I would test them to the limit and even when I would scream and shout at them they would just smile at me. They never seemed to lose their temper and were always happy. Tommy and I were glad to have them as our sound crew, but I began to keep my distance, I didn't want to become like these 'born-again Christians'. I thought that they never had any fun. After the gigs they'd pack up the sound system and go straight back to the hotel. That wasn't for me! I was far too busy enjoying my life, or so I thought. Anyway they didn't have what I had, I had so much 'fun' drinking, fighting and women. In truth, they had so much more than me. They were secure and didn't need these things. They knew the truth and it gave them peace of mind.

Gradually I began to hate the life I was living. I hated the drinking every night, it was becoming a habit I couldn't shake, and I hated everything it led to. I couldn't stop. I was too far down the road. I tried reading the Bible. Why? I don't know, perhaps I was trying to find some answers, or maybe trying to find God then, but to be truthful it was no use, even that didn't bring me any solace. I felt so guilty, but even when I did I somehow managed to shove these feelings to the back of my mind. Yet somewhere deep inside me I knew that I had to face up to what I was doing, to face God. But then again, I reasoned to myself, I was no different to any other man on the street, apart from these Christians. I reasoned that I hadn't really done anything wrong, I was generous and hadn't stolen anything, I was quite sure that God would forgive me these 'little things' when I was dead. How foolish!

During the winter of 1986, we returned for the Christmas season once again to Bradford and as usual my old friend Max Wigley came in to see me. It was great to see him and now we could have more discussions and arguments about the Christian message. I asked him many questions and he answered them very simply. In fact, what he told me made me realize that God was a real Person. What you must realize was that to me then, God was only a force, or a distant figure found only in the Bible or church or Sunday school. God was for people who didn't have anything else in their lives. I told Max that now my daughter was growing up I was becoming very embarrassed about watching even PG rated films with her, because of the bad language and innuendo's, I also raised questions about the state of the world and said I hoped Jesus was real as He would be the only One who could sort it out. Max told me later that he could see Jesus already working in my life, but at that time I wasn't interested in becoming a 'born-again Christian', it was the furthest thing from my mind. Max and I had quite a few talks and the more we talked, the more my guilt would come to the surface. A few days later Max came to see me and said that he felt we should have a talk. It was about an hour before the curtain went up, so we sat down and what he told me next changed my life forever. He told me about the love and justice of God, using this illustration;

'One day a judge came into court wearing his fine robes and wig and sat in his elevated chair behind his big bench. He looked at the dock, and there in the dock was his own son, whom he loved very much and wanted to forgive for all the sins he had committed. However, as a judge he had to be just and needed to hear the case against his son. He listened as his son's sins were read out before the court and after hearing, pronounced his son guilty and fined him £500. He then took off his wig and his fine robes and came down from his bench and walked across the floor of the court. He took his cheque book out, signed a cheque for £500 and paid the fine for his son.'

Max pointed out that the judge had been both loving and just and that is what God has done for us through Jesus Christ. I realized that Max was telling me that God knows we have broken His laws and that we deserve to be punished, but He also loves us enough to come Himself and take the punishment that we deserve.

This illustration had a great effect on me; I had never looked at God that way. It made him seem more real. I knew that I had to be forgiven for what I had done and coming before God as the judge's son had done in the illustration seemed the only way. I looked at Max and told him that I wanted to become a Christian that night but because we were ready to go on stage would he wait until the end of the show. He agreed and left to visit other artiste in their dressing rooms. The curtain went up and everyone got on with the business of putting a show on, except me, because all the way through the show I couldn't get Max, and all that he had told me, out of my mind. Had I said the right thing? Did I really want to become a Christian or was I kidding myself? Was I ready to become one? I felt that I had done the wrong thing by saying that I didn't want to become a Christian, because I felt I wasn't good enough to be one, I felt I had sinned too much. It was strange because when I though about God I felt dirty and un-worthy of his love. I also felt that if I committed to God and he was real then I was sure I would let him down. It's not that I didn't want to get to know the Lord; it's just that my way of life had become a sort of drug to me, with all the adulation and excess that fame brings. I also knew that if I got know the Lord, and knowing my personality, I would have to tell everyone, and that would lead to everyone laughing at me and ridiculing me. I didn't know if I could handle that. I felt very frightened and threatened. I realize now that it was the devil that was making me feel threatened, because he knew I was about to walk in God's presence and he didn't want to lose a good disciple.

After the curtain came down I went to my dressing fully expecting Max to be there, but luckily for me he wasn't. He was in some other dressing-room talking to another member of the cast. I got busy preparing some lie or other to tell so that I could get out of this situation when he walked in. I have never felt so frightened in my life. Max told me later that I was deathly white and looked visibly shaken. I felt I was in the presence of God. The room was filled with an over-whelming sense of peace. I now know that the peace I was feeling was coming from the Holy Spirit that was following Max around like an old friend. I know in my heart that I couldn't face God because I felt so un-worthy and ashamed, so I took the coward's way out and asked Max if we could leave things and I would come and see him when we had a matinee. That day God was waiting for me and I turned my face away from him, what a clown I was, I should have grabbed the opportunity with both hands, but God is always there, it just took me longer. Max just smiled at me and said it was okay and that I could come and see him anytime. He knew God was working in my life and that it was only a matter of time before I accepted him as my Lord and Savior.

I went home that night a very troubled man. I knew I had to face the Lord and I wanted too, but it seemed such a big step. It seemed as if I was about to jump over the edge of the Grand Canyon into the un-known. I had been in control of everything and this felt like I was in control of nothing. I felt so frightened. This is where trusting in the Lord kicks in. I didn't want to become a monk or a 'holier-than-thou' kind of person. I just wanted to stay me! Only without the sinning, but most of all I wanted to be forgiven. I wrestled with my conscience for a few days, with the devil clinging on to me, but in the back of my mind I knew inevitably what would happen. I didn't tell Yvonne about all the turmoil my mind was going through, even though I had spoken about God and the bible many times to her in the past. This was something between me and the Lord. I kept wrestling with my conscience, telling myself that I was doing fine and that I didn't need Him in my life. But it was too no avail, I knew I had to contact Max and talk to him at length about it.

A few days later I telephoned Max and told him that I would like to come over and talk to him. He told me that that would be no problem, and it was arranged that I would go and see him at his vicarage the following day. I rang Trevor and told him that he would have to run me over to Max's the next day. It went quiet at the other end of the line, and then I heard him say quietly 'Ok'. He didn't ask why but just accepted it. I think by now he had become used to me and thought it was just another crazy scheme that I was up too. If only he knew how this would change my life. I then told Yvonne I was going to see Max the following day. She asked me why and I told her that I wanted to see him because I was interested in knowing more about God. If only she had known that inside I was petrified in case I actually got to meet God.

The next day came and Trev and I set off for Bradford to see Max. Instead of chattering all the time I was very quiet on the journey, which is not at all like me. Trevor must have been wondering what was wrong. What he didn't know was that I felt I was stepping into something that was beyond my control. I didn't know what was going to happen, but I knew I would be talking about God as I had never spoken about Him before. We arrived at Max's house and Trevor walked with me to the door. He didn't wait with me; he was off like a rocket. Max came to the door and asked me in. I was beginning to feel very strange. I thought to myself, why am I doing this? We went through to Max's study and he asked if I wanted a cup of tea. I would have sooner been in a pub having a whiskey but for some reason I stayed. Max and I talked a little about nothing and then he started to talk about God. He then produced a little book called 'Journey into Life. He asked if I would like him to read it me and I said yes. Do you know, I can't even remember what the book was all about, but all I know is after Max had finished reading it, I knew I had to give my life to the Lord. Sorry, I will re-phrase that. I WANTED to give my life to the Lord. I turned to Max and told that I didn't know what was happening to me but I wanted to become a Christian, whatever that meant. Without any prompting from Max I was on my knees, something I had never done even as a child. At the end of the booklet there was a little prayer and Max asked me if I would like to say it. I didn't know it then but it was a sinner's prayer, (a prayer that asks God for forgiveness) I told him I would and began to say the prayer. I only got halfway through and found I couldn't say anymore. Tears began to fill my eyes and I started to cry like a baby. I felt a glow, a warmth, spread from the top of my head right the way through my body. I knew at that moment the Lord was real, as real as you or me. And, not only that, I knew that in His mercy, He had forgiven me. I felt clean and alive for the first time in my life. I got a wonderful feeling of exhilaration, a feeling of belonging to God. I felt special. Nothing else mattered to me, only being with the Lord. Through my tears I asked Max to finish the prayer for me. I didn't even listen. I was too busy thanking the Lord for saving me. I can't begin to tell you all that I felt, but when God puts His hand on you and loves you there's no feeling like it in this world. I knew that my life had changed and that I was at the start of a new journey.

I know that a lot of people say it's a load of rubbish, and I was one of them, but I'm here to tell you today that finding the Lord is the only way to live, it is impossible without Him. It wasn't only an emotional experience; it went much further than that. Some have said to me that when people go to a church or a gospel meeting and make a decision to be born-again Christians it is because of the atmosphere and the minister whipping them up into an emotional frenzy, but I found the Lord in a little room of a vicarage, with just one other person and me quietly talking about Jesus Christ. So it doesn't matter where you are, if you truly want the Lord to come into your life, He will. It doesn't matter who you are, you just have to ask! He is such a gracious and merciful God that He won't come into your life unless you ask Him in.

I thanked Max for helping me to find the Lord and bade him goodbye. When I arrived back at the car Trevor was there waiting. I got in and told him that I'd found the Lord. He gave me a strange look and eventually said,

'I'm happy for you, but don't try to push it on me.' It made me laugh, suddenly I had become an alien, but do you know, it felt good. All the way home, I didn't speak once, I just wanted to stay in this new found peace that the Lord had given me. All my questions about God over the years were now being answered very clearly. I was walking on air. It was the biggest high I have ever had, bigger than when we topped the bill at the Opera House, Blackpool for ten weeks to 360,000 people, bigger than being the subjects of the TV programme, *'This is your life,'* even bigger than when we met the Queen. This was the biggest thing that had ever happened to me. I knew God personally, and everything else pales into insignificance after that.

I eventually arrived home and broke the news to Yvonne that I had found God and had become a born-again Christian. As I was telling her what had happened I started to cry again because I was so happy. I cried for three days. I was weeping tears of joy and felt extremely emotional that by Gods mercy I had been forgiven. She looked at me strangely and said she was happy for me, but later on told me that she had thought it was a fad and sooner or later I would get over it. I'm certain that a lot of people thought the same, but I am here to tell you that since that time in 1986 I am still the same 'lover of God'. I now had a peace about me that I am quite sure must have seemed strange to Yvonne and those who knew me, this was nothing like the 'quality of life' episode, I couldn't manufacture this myself, it was all by the power of the Holy Spirit.

As soon as I had finished telling Yvonne about how I had met with the Lord, I looked at her and she seemed different to me. For the first time in many years I really looked at my wife, and this time I was looking at her through Christian eyes. I saw inside her, gentleness and kindness and how much she had loved me and stood by me all these years. I felt so much love for her that it seemed to overwhelm me. God was giving me back my marriage, He was taking away the selfishness and replacing it with a love which was much more I'd ever experienced. He gave me a love for my fellow man, and Yvonne is much more to me than a fellow man, so you can imagine the love I had begun to feel for her. God had given me a true marriage.

For the next few weeks I did nothing but talk about God and how wonderful He is. He seemed to fill every waking hour. Yvonne must have thought she was living with a different man, because I never lost my temper and didn't swear, I was at a total peace within myself. Of course, I was a different man. I was brand new, reborn and now understood the truth about life. And the truth is; you just can't live a consistently good life without God. I told my family and my friends about being saved and they accepted it without any qualms, a few friends took the Mickey out of me, but I didn't care because after what they did to Jesus, a few people having a laugh at my expense seemed very trivial. After a few days of living with this different man, Yvonne said she wanted what I had. I was over the moon, now I thought that Yvonne and I would be together in Gods love. I telephoned Max and told him what Yvonne had said and that she wanted to give her heart to the Lord. He asked me if I was sure and I told him I was. My enthusiasm knew no bounds. I didn't understand then that it is the heart that must want the Lord and not just the brain. I now know that He goes straight to the source of our true feelings, the heart.

Max came to us. He dutifully arrived later that afternoon and we all got on our knees to pray to the Lord. After we had finished I looked at Yvonne hoping to see God within her, but she seemed no different from before. She told me later that she didn't feel any different, but she thought that was how Christians should feel. For me, having had such a strong experience of God, it seemed impossible that anyone could just sit there and say that they were now a Christian without showing any further emotion. I asked Max if he thought Yvonne had found the Lord, but he just replied that God works in many different ways with different people. We thanked Max for coming over and said our goodbyes. I watched Yvonne for tell-tale signs of salvation, but I was very disappointed to find that she hadn't changed in any way. I didn't realize that God was already working underneath in her life, and that it was just a matter of time. This was just the first step, that's all. I saw that God does not save everyone in the same way, He knows us more than we do and works with the individual in the way that is best for them. I realize now that although Yvonne had made the decision to give her life to God in her mind, the time would come when she would give her whole heart to the Lord and then He would be able to change her life and give her all the healing, peace and gifts He has promised to all who come to Him.

A couple of months later we had to go on tour. Now it was different, no longer did I want to tour alone, I wanted Yvonne with me all the time. It wasn't that I was frightened of being tempted, because God had already healed me in that area of my life and now I had no desire for anyone other than my wife, but I wanted Yvonne with me because I loved her so much and wanted to make up for all those lost years.

It was strange, but wonderful on the tour. Now that I the Lord with me I looked at everything differently. No longer did I want to run around discos, I had fulfilment, I just wanted to be with Yvonne. It was wonderful that after the show we would go out for meals together and share our lives instead of her being at one end of the country and me at the other.

About two weeks into the tour we arrived at Margate. It was a dismal day with the clouds hanging low over the horizon, which gave the town an atmosphere of foreboding. It would turn out to be a day unlike any other. The evening came and Tommy and I as usual went to our dressing rooms and got ready for the show. We went on stage to a full house that night and so there was a feeling of excitement running around backstage. The sound company, Wigwam, had been in all day doing their stuff and setting up the equipment, and now that I was a born-again Christian, they felt more like brothers to me than just a company who worked with us. Tommy and I went on stage and did well. When we came off Yvonne was waiting for me,

'I must see Mike Spratt,' she said, very determined, she seemed a little agitated but I knew that the only possible reason for her to want to see Mike would be to talk to him about God. What Yvonne didn't realize was that when a touring show ends, it is then than the real work begins. The backstage boys have to pull down all the lights and sound equipment, load them into trucks and then set off to wherever the next show is. The pulling down of the equipment can take anywhere from one to three hours depending on the size of the rig they are using, and we used a big rig. I tried in the best way possible to explain all this to Yvonne, but she was adamant. She had to see him now, she said. Well, I was not about to get in Gods way! The audience had gone, so I rushed down into the auditorium and found Mike pulling some gear down.

'Mike,' I said, watching him as he worked hard, 'Yvonne wants to see you, I think she wants to talk about the Lord.'

He stared at me with a hopeless look in his eyes.

'I really haven't got time at the minute, Bob,' he replied. 'I have to get all this gear out.'

'Never mind the gear, Mike,' I said. 'What about your duty to God?'

He looked at me and smiled, 'You're right.'

He stopped what he was doing and we both set off for

the dressing-room to see Yvonne. Mike asked Yvonne what it was she wanted to see him about, but she said she wanted to see him on her own, privately. The dressing room by this time was full with people, some visiting, some taking things out, some just hanging around, it was chaotic. So Yvonne and Mike went off together in search of a quiet room.

They were gone for about half an hour, but when Yvonne walked back into my room, it was the most wonderful sight I had ever seen. She was literally glowing with the Holy Spirit. She had been born-again. I looked at her and said,

'You've just found God haven't you, Yvonne?'

She just smiled and nodded. I was full of questions.

'You know the truth now don't you, Yvonne?' I asked, my enthusiasm running at an all time high.

'Oh yes.' She replied, her eyes nearly closing.

'Well, how do you feel, Yvonne?' I asked. I was like a child.

She looked at me with a patience that I had not seen in her before.

'All I know Bob,' she said, 'is that God is very real.'

I could tell that I was asking too many questions, and she just wanted to be quiet and not have the feeling of peace inside her disturbed with my incessant questioning. I didn't ask any more, but it was murder for me to keep my cool because I wanted to jump for joy! Now that we were both Christians, we could live together for eternity. What a wonderful God we have! Now no longer did she think it was all just a fad, now she herself knew the truth and we could now walk our Journey with Christ, together.

Another funny thing happened that night which Yvonne and I have chuckled about ever since. When she accepted Jesus into her life and she was saved, she was so completely overcome with joy that, with tears running down her face, she flung her arms around Mike and gave him a big hug, he hugged her back, obviously delighted at what had just happened and at that very moment the door of the room burst open and in came a member of the crew, who wasn't a Christian. We could just imagine what would have gone through his mind. There was Bobby Ball's wife and Mike Spratt hugging each other in a deserted dressing room, hidden away at the back of the theatre. He lowered his eyes and backed out of the room. We just knew that soon there would be a rumour running around the theatre that Yvonne and Mike Spratt were having an affair, and that 'poor Bobby' knew nothing about it. Well, I did, and it was the best type of 'affair' she could have!

Before I became a Christian, I hadn't really given much thought to the devil, because I hadn't truly believed in the Lord so how could I believe in the devil? But I have to tell you that he is real, even if he has been defeated by Jesus, he still looks around for someone to trash. After Yvonne and I became Christians, the enemy of our souls must have realized that he had lost two good disciples, because it wasn't long before he began to attack us. Things happened to us that if the Lord hadn't been with us would have cracked us up. Nobody could fully understand what we went through, but it was horrible. But we praise the Lord God, for it proves how much He must love us for the devil to attack us in the way he did.

I feel that I have to tell you Yvonne's story and the Lord's strength in case anyone who reads this book is going through the same thing, and perhaps it will help them.

Yvonne has been an epileptic all of her life, and about twelve months before I became a Christian, the fits she suffered became a little worse. She only had mild epilepsy and maybe had one major fit a year and mild blackouts, but now she began to have more. As a child she only had the blackouts but then began to have fits when she reached her teens, she pushed it all to the back of her mind and ignored them, not admitting to having them, she felt there was a stigma attached. Her epilepsy made her feel different to others, which of course she is not, and neither is any other epileptic. I knew of Yvonne's epilepsy when we married but she told me at the last minute because she was terrified that I would walk out on her, but I have a niece who suffers much worse from epilepsy so it made no difference to me in the slightest. (In fact, I think that the government should launch a campaign on epilepsy so everyone can have the right information about those who suffer from epilepsy and they would not be treated like lepers, as they quite often feel.) I love my wife with all my heart for all that she is.

Yvonne hadn't needed to take any medication for many years and so, as things began to worsen we talked about her going to see a specialist about what she could do to help. She reluctantly agreed, not wanting any medication, and we went off to see him. He examined her and prescribed some tablets which were supposed to control the epilepsy, and they did, but the side effects, which weren't fully explained to us, were horrendous. We weren't Christians as yet, so didn't come before God in prayer to ask for the right way to go about this. Over the next twelve months Yvonne gradually began to change. It happened so slowly that I didn't even notice. To tell you the truth, I'm not sure I would have noticed anyway, because at that time I was too interested in my own career. She became very withdrawn and lost interest in food. Before long her weight began to drop and she couldn't sleep at night which led to a misuse of sleeping tablets and these plus the epilepsy medication left her constantly lethargic. She was like a zombie. When you live with someone, you are usually the last one to notice the changes. The change is so gradual that it creeps up on you slowly and it is accepted as a normal way of living. This is what happened to Yvonne and me. Yvonne was very very ill, but somehow managed to hide it from me. She told me later that she hid her feelings from me because she thought I had enough on my mind without having her to worry about as well. I couldn't tell what was going on in Yvonne's mind at that time in our lives but I did notice the extreme weight loss. I began to nag her about it, telling her to eat more and she promised she would, but of course, that put her off food more. When we went out for a meal she would eat a small amount and then place her serviette over her plate so that no-one would notice how little she had eaten. She wouldn't make herself sick or anything, but if I bullied her into eating more than she could handle she would have to race to the bathroom to vomit, her stomach just couldn't cope with large amounts of food. She would, in contrast, feed Joanne and me absolutely huge platefuls of food and tell us that she had already eaten by the time we came to sit and eat.

During this time the press began to turn against Tom and me. Anything we did on TV, good or bad, they slated it. Even live performances were not safe from them. We went to a club in the Midlands and one newspaper sent a reporter to see us. He didn't introduce himself to us but just sat in the audience to watch our act. That night we got a full standing ovation for about four minutes. We stormed them. But the reporter didn't report that. The next day in the newspaper he wrote that we were the worst act he had ever seen (or words to that effect). He had just reported his own feelings and failed to mention what the other 99 per cent of the audience had thought. Another time Tom and I were doing a lavish pantomime in the London Palladium. There were lots of other stars on the bill with us like Barbara Windsor and Rod Hull to name but two and the box office had already taken £300,000 in the opening week. It was a record. According to the promoter, over one million pounds had been spent on the sets and costumes so it looked as though it would be a roaring success. It was one of the most spectacular shows Tommy and I have ever had the honour of being in. On the opening night, the show was terrific, everyone had worked so hard and we were all pleased how well it had gone. But in the audience was one man who was a leading critic for a top newspaper. The next day in the newspaper he gave us the biggest blasting possible. They don't call them critics for no reason and that's just what he did, he criticized the sets, the costumes the performers, in fact I don't think there was one thing he didn't criticize. But the truth of the story, (and not a lot of people know this) that he was sitting in his seat sound asleep from the beginning of the panto until the end. I know this for certain because Yvonne was sitting opposite the aisle from him, and watched him all night. He saw nothing of the pantomime. This was the type of thing Tom and I were having to put up with at that time and it can be so demoralizing when you work so hard and do well in front of the majority and one person goes out and systematically tries to ruin your career. To be truthful I don't know exactly what a critic does except criticize things, it's a sad job really. Why don't they encourage, build up and compliment? I personally don't think anyone has the right to criticize what they cannot do themselves. Mind you, if they could do whatever it is they are criticizing, they wouldn't need to be a critic.

Another major disappointment we suffered was at the hands of our own profession. I had only been a Christian for a few months when we were asked if we would perform at the annual Water Rats ball. The Water Rats are a closed society made up of those in show business people, they do some good works for charity and you would have to be approached before being allowed to join. Both Tommy and I had once hoped to be asked to join and so it was quite an honour for us to be asked to be the cabaret at their ball. It was a very sophisticated affair, with all the gentlemen in bow ties and the ladies in ball gowns. As the day came closer we got very excited. There was to be no payment for this gig, but nevertheless, we put in our own orchestra at our own expense, we really wanted to entertain them and who knows, we'd thought, they may even ask us in. I will never forget that night as long as I live. The ball was being held at the Grosvenor Hotel, so Tommy and I were to change in one of the rooms. When it came time to go on we were a bundle of nerves. The band played our opening music and we were on. I looked out into the audience and saw many faces from TV, and magazines. It was such an honour to be working to our fellow performers. What happened next became a nightmare. No-one laughed, they refused to. We went down like a lead balloon; there was nothing, no encouragement, nothing. I couldn't understand it then, and still don't see how members of my own profession could watch us die like that. It's not even as though we were being paid, it was for them and it was for charity. We tried to get through it but it got more difficult as we went along, some of them looked at us as though we were a disease. It was clear that they had purposely done this, by now they had turned their backs on us and were talking with each other louder than we were talking on stage. Eventually we came off and made our way back to the room. None of us could speak, we were heartbroken. How could this happen. How could performers not clap his fellow performers? It was something alien to Tommy and me. All the years we had been in show business we had thought it was a family. Well if it is, then that night proved that we weren't part of it. That episode left me deeply wary of all these secret societies, and I found out the hard way that there are some in the business who will love everything you do to your face, but just as quickly will turn on you the moment someone else does.

Meanwhile, Yvonne was getting steadily worse. The devil was having a field day. The day came when Yvonne admitted that she was feeling very depressed, so we went back to see the doctor. When we got there, Yvonne told the doctor her symptoms. He then got out a book and looked up the side effects of the tablets which he had prescribed her, it was unbelievable, no-one had mentioned any side effects to us. The tablets had caused all these problems so I told him in no uncertain terms that I was taking her off the tablets as she was better off without them. He then dropped a bombshell. He informed us that if we went ahead with that, Yvonne would suffer multiple seizures and would end up in hospital with brain damage. We just sat there, stunned, we didn't know what to do. I felt that if we had been warned about the side effects before Yvonne had begun to take these pills, I wouldn't have pushed her so much into taking them. I felt that it was all my fault. I had changed my Yvonne from a woman who laughed a lot into a woman who was withdrawn and living a nightmare.

The doctor told us that the only way we could prevent all this and any further damage was to gradually wean her off the tablets and go onto some different, milder ones. We decided that was what we would do, we could not let this carry on, she could not lose any more weight, she had already become extremely thin and looked anorexic. We set off home determined to get her well again. It was during this period that I found the Lord, and now I had His help; there was nothing we couldn't do.

That summer season, Tommy and I were working at Paignton, Devon and by this time we had weaned Yvonne off the epilepsy tablets. So when season time came around I set off for Paignton and Yvonne stayed at home as Joanne was still at school. About three weeks into the season I got a call saying that she had to come down to see me. I knew something was seriously wrong, so I told her to get a taxi there and then and come down to me. When she arrived she was in a terrible state. I have never seen her looking so bad. She was five foot ten and weighed seven stone three. Now that's thin! As I said before, you can live with someone and not notice anything wrong until the last minute, because the change is so gradual, but now I noticed. I knew that only with the Lords help could we get her well. I sat her down and told her to tell me everything. She told me that she feared she had anorexia (caused by the tablets) and that she was hooked on sleeping tablets. I asked her how many sleeping pills she took each night and she said she was embarrassed about it but it was usually four but could sometimes be up to eight a night. I couldn't believe what I was hearing. Yvonne at the time took the strongest sleeping tablet which was prescribed, and she took four plus a night. And the doctor just kept on prescribing them seemingly by the bucket-load! (By this time Yvonne had also become a Christian, so the situation wasn't hopeless.) I told her that when the evening came she wasn't to take any sleeping tablets at all and if she couldn't sleep, she mustn't worry about it, because I'd stay up with her all night if I had to. I was so naïve to think it would be this easy. We went to bed and said our goodnights and tried to go to sleep. After about an hour Yvonne was up, she couldn't sleep and began to scratch every part of her body. She was having withdrawal symptoms. She was crying and saying her body was driving her crazy. I felt hopeless; all that I could do was sit there and love her. I realized then that this was going to be a long journey, but I was determined that we would succeed. I couldn't bear to watch her go through the agony any longer and gave Yvonne a couple of sleeping tablets and told her we would begin to work things out in the morning.

When morning came, I believe the Lord had given me

an answer. I told Yvonne that we would wean her off the sleeping tablets, just as we had the epilepsy tablets. I said that we would give her less and less and space them out and so on until she was no longer dependant on them. She agreed with me and that night took her first steps to recovery. One night I asked her to meet me at the theatre after the show, because we had been invited to go out for a few drinks with friends. For some reason she reluctantly agreed and met me after the curtain went down. We met up with our friends and went across the road to a hotel frequented by all the other acts from shows in town. We stayed for about an hour and then left. When we got outside Yvonne came over very ill. I asked her if she had been drinking too much, I was convinced she must have been drinking, and with her hardly eating it wouldn't have taken her long to become drunk. She was so upset and explained that she hadn't drank anything stronger that coffee, I hadn't seen her with a drink either and so I realized there must be something else. She went on to explain that whenever she left the house she suffered panic attacks and felt as though she was choking. She said that she never wanted to leave the house, because it was torture for her to go out. She also said that she didn't usually feel so bad if she was with me, but if she was on her own it was one of the most difficult things she had to do. Now for me, someone who had never experienced this, it was very difficult to understand.

We got back to the house and Yvonne poured out her heart to me. She told me all of her insecurities and fears and everything that had gone wrong in her life. I realized that I had a part in sapping the strength of a very strong woman over the years and now she desperately needed some of mine. A lot of the time we are quite foolish with the ones we love. Now I looked at her and saw a very frightened little girl. This was the mother of my daughter, the woman who meant more to me than life itself, and I along with other things had reduced her to this, by taking her for granted, to a woman who was hooked on sleeping tablets, an anorexic and agoraphobic. I knew now that we had to pray like we never had before, and we did! The Lord then started His marvelous work.

That night I lay awake talking away to God, asking what I could do. I got no audible answer, and it felt as though He wasn't answering anything. It's strange, you know, but sometimes when we think that the Lord isn't listening, it's at those times when He's working the hardest for us. The next day I set off to the theatre without an answer to our problems, but as the old saying goes, 'the Lord works in mysterious ways' because on the way there, I passed a field and in the middle of it was a tree, and under the tree was a bench. I stopped the car and looked at the sight in front of my eyes. I knew right away what the answer was. The Lord had answered my prayers. He showed me through this picture that Yvonne didn't need medication; all she needed was the love of the Lord and love I could give her as a supportive husband. I went home that night feeling very hopeful about the future. I no longer cared about my career or anything else for that matter, all that mattered to me was Yvonne. She had taken over my life as my main priority and that's just how I wanted it. I told her about the tree in the field and explained that we were going through this together and would take it day by day. I took charge and told her that we must have a plan, and the plan was that we would stay in one day and that we would go out the next and sit under the tree for an hour. We would slowly build up the time she spent out of the house as we went along. She agreed with me and with God's help we started on our way to recovery. It wasn't easy. It was, in fact, one of the hardest times we have ever been through. Every so often we would call into a little church opposite to where we were staying and say a few prayers before we set off to sit under our tree. It was strange really, each day we were taking the agoraphobia step by step and each night we dealt with the dependency on sleeping tablets step by step. No one really knows what we went through. But with the Lord's help we fought the devil and won.

Every other day we would sit under our tree, holding hands and praying and slowly but surely Yvonne began to regain her strength. After weeks of doing this she had beaten her dependency on sleeping tablets, and now was able to get a true nights' sleep. During the middle of all this something happened to me that even now I find hard to forget. Every season with Tommy's help I would organize a charity Rock and Roll show, all the proceeds would go to a local charity and we all got together and had a wonderful time. We had been doing this for years, so it had become normal to get one together each year and this year was no different. This year a very well-known comedian, (who will remain anonymous) was topping the bill in a theatre in nearby Torquay, and I ran into him one night in a local club, where I was discussing a venue for the charity night. I thought that while I had the chance I would ask him if he would do our charity night. We knew each other very well so I thought it would be no problem to ask him. I walked over to him and tapped him on the shoulder. I wasn't prepared for what greeted me. He turned around and glared at me as though he hated me. I ignored the look and asked him if he would do the charity. He came closer to me and we stood nose to nose. He was a very big star and usually had a few bodyguards with him, tonight was no exception. They all stood behind him just waiting for him to do something. He must have thought he was intimidating me but he was wrong. I began to feel all the old anger build up inside. He told me with pure hate in his eyes that I would be the last person he would do a charity for. I asked him why and he told me that he didn't like me and then asked me what I was going to do about it. My anger was now full blown and I could almost hear the devil urging me on. I just wanted to knock him out there and then, just to show him that he didn't scare me and neither did his bodyguards. I was about to fly at him but something stopped me. I thought of Jesus and suddenly found myself wondering what He would do in this situation. I swallowed my anger and said to him that I was sorry that he didn't like me and that if I had done anything to upset him in the past, I hoped that he could find it in his heart to forgive me. I then turned on my heel and walked away.

I stayed on at the club a little longer at the club to sort out the arrangements for the charity then I went home. I felt strange, inside the devil was telling me that I was a coward, and that I should have been strong and beaten him up, but I knew deep down that I had done the right thing. By having self-control I was much stronger. I was now a Christian and I had just done what the Lord would have wanted me to do. I told the devil to go away in no uncertain terms and then went back and told Yvonne what had happened. She was so proud of me and told me that now I was a real man. She knew just what I had been like before I became a Christian, I would have hit him, but now the Lord had taught me that the violence belonged to the devil and it had no place in my life anymore.

He didn't come to the charity and continued to avoid me. Then when the season was almost over I saw him again in the club. I had my back to him and was talking to some of my family who were there when I felt a tap on my shoulder. I turned around and it was him. He asked me how the charity had gone down. Well, it was a very strange situation; here was this man who a few weeks previously had arrogantly intimidated me, now asking me humbly how the charity had gone. I took him by the arm and led him away from everyone. He probably thought I was going to have a go at him, but that was the furthest thing from my mind. I asked him what the problem was, and he told me that he had noticed that I was a different man from the one I used to be. I replied truthfully that I knew that because now I had God looking after me. I could tell by his eyes that he didn't understand what that statement meant, so I asked him what his reasons were for disliking me. He told me that a few years before I had bitten his ear in a club in London and that I had made it bleed.

'Oh, is that all?' I said.

I then proceeded to put him on the floor and playfully pretended to bite his ear, only this time being careful not to draw any blood! We laughed and that night walked away from one another with a friendship and a new respect. I saw then that he was just like I had been, and wasn't truly happy. He has since shown an interest in God and I hope that one day he will make a firm decision to follow Jesus. Only the Lord can truly help him.

By the end of the season Yvonne was definitely on the mend. We had got over her addiction to sleeping tablets and by this time she was sleeping soundly without them which I believe would have taken much longer and been much harder for her to do without much prayer and focusing on God. Much slower, though, was the battle with agoraphobia, but by now she was able to go out with me without having any panic attacks. She was still extremely thin, but I knew she could only get better and the trick was not to nag her to eat, which would only put her off, so too watching every morsel she put in her mouth. I just let her go at her own steady pace and kept my eye on how much she was eating, trying to be as gentle as I could. I only had to think of our lives before we were Christians, Yvonne had a husband she could never fully trust, she never knew when I was coming home and she never knew when I was going to explode in a fit of anger. It's no wonder she was an emotional wreck. But every day through the season we prayed and slowly she began to get well.

We were weary after the summer season, but at least we were winning. One day we went to the village and I stayed in the car while Yvonne did some shopping. I seemed to have been waiting only a few moments before she came back. I was surprised and asked her what was wrong. She told me everything was fine and that she had got the things she needed. I thought no more of it until the following week when we went into the village again. During the time Yvonne had been ill, she had tried to hide all her emotions from me. But this time I had become very suspicious of her lightning fast shopping trips. So the next time we went I decided to follow her. I was amazed to see her run in and out of the shops as though she was on fire. She didn't know I was watching her so when she arrived back at the car I was already waiting. I asked why she had run around the shops instead of walking, and told her that I had seen her. She then admitted to me that she still suffered the panic attacks. She ran because there was no way she could have walked around the shops. I told her that the next time we went I was going to try something.

The following week came and we set off to the village. I parked my car at the top of the high street and told Yvonne that I would be watching her as she did her shopping. Not in a creepy domineering kind of way, you understand, but to be a support to her as she was by now fine when she was out with me. I was parked on double yellow lines and I could tell that inside Yvonne was panicking, because she used this as an excuse, along with others, not to go.

'You can't park here,' she said, 'you might get a ticket.'

I told her not to worry about it and after much persuasion she set off down the high street to do her shopping. Slowly I followed her in the car, and every time she began to run, I called out, 'Walk Yvonne!' This seemed to have the desired effect, because she began to slow down and actually walked. We did this quite a few times. Yvonne said that it was alright if someone else was there, but there was no way she could do it on her own. She was fine if she went shopping with our Mavis or if I was following her in the car, but otherwise she stayed in the house.

This went on for a couple of months and then one morning I got up out of bed and Yvonne wasn't in the house. This was out of character for her, but I wasn't too worried as I reasoned that she was probably out with our Mavis. I made myself a cup of tea and settled down to read the newspaper. I had been there for a couple of minutes when I heard a car pull up outside. I looked up and saw it was a taxi. Yvonne got out alone, paid the taxi fare and came into the house. Her face was blooming; she looked like the cat that got the cream. She sat down and told me that she had just walked around the village on her own, fine. She looked so proud of herself, and I was so proud of her too. She went on to tell me that she had got out of bed that morning feeling depressed and so had prayed to the Lord for help. She felt an urge, like He was telling her to go out to the village on her own. She said she had been so afraid but had plucked up the courage and had done it. When she got there, she immediately felt the old panic attacks creeping up on her but somehow managed to control them. She finished her story and sat back glowing. She knew she had broken through a barrier and taken a step forward. I really believe that instead of me or our Mavis walking with Yvonne that morning, the Lord Himself had gone with her. I can honestly say that I believe God had said enough was enough, and that He was going to take over, all she had to do was ask and trust that He would answer her.

From then on Yvonne began to improve. Over the next two years she became stronger and stronger and was soon back to her normal weight, and no longer suffered any panic attacks. She is, through God's grace, a stronger woman now than she has ever been in her life.

Becoming a Christian and finding the Lord (although I find that funny as He has never been lost), is the best and most important thing that has ever happened to me. He has done so much within my life, reshaping me and rebuilding me. Through Him I have good Christian friends whom I can trust; Mike Spratt, Ray Bevan, Chris Gidney and of course Max Wigley also my friend and Pastor, Mario Mariani. I don't wish to leave anyone out, but I have found friends through the Lord too numerous to mention. At one time I would have shied away from these people, thinking they must be boring, but they are the most interesting people I know. They don't want to be friends with you for what you can give them, or for what you are, but because they are true brothers. I know that these people would never let me down or gossip about me, or stab me in the back, they encourage and help and if I need correcting, they would do it in love. The most important thing is that I could trust them with my life. So thank you everyone, just for being there.

Not long after we had become Christians, Yvonne and I decided together that we wanted to be baptized. I strongly felt I had to make some sort of public commitment to God. When I spoke to Yvonne about it, she asked me what it would involve, so I said I would ask our local church at that time, Heywood Baptist Church, all about it. Mike also went to this church then so I asked him if it would be okay for us to be baptized there and he said it would. I asked him all about it and He told me that we would need some old clothes and something to change into after the baptism. I relayed what he had told me to Yvonne and she agreed that it was something we had to do so we set a date for the baptism. I will never forget that day as long as I live. We set out for the church with our change of clothes under our arms, wondering what was going to happen. When we arrived, the minister, Mike Hook, took us to a back room and began to explain. I could see Yvonne slowly turning white. Mike told us he would call out our names and we would have to stand up in front of the (packed) church and speak into the microphone and tell the congregation how we came to be Christians. Then we would have to make our way down to where we were to be baptized, get into the water, where two men would lay us back and submerge us fully under. Yvonne immediately panicked as a) there was no way she could stand up and talk in front of all those people; and b) she couldn't swim, so to be submerged backwards underwater would be a frightening experience. In contrast, I was fine because I'm a strong swimmer and talking in front of people on a microphone is my job. But at that moment, Yvonne had the problem. She was in the midst of getting over everything at the time and so really began to panic. Mike Hook said not to worry because everything would be alright.

We sat down in the church and began to pray. It's a funny thing, but sometimes even as Christians we still all find it difficult to give everything to the Lord. It's a good job we did that night. Yvonne and I just sat there praying like mad as Mike Hook began to call out the names of those who were to be baptized. Yvonne was gripping my hand and it felt as though she was going to break it, then suddenly my name was called. I looked at Yvonne and she looked so vulnerable, but before I knew it I was on my way to the front of the church. If you ask me to explain fully what happened next, I couldn't, all I can say is while I was on my way down the aisle, the Holy Spirit filled me so I felt as though I would burst. The tears began to stream down my face and it felt as if I was being re-born again! By the time I reached the microphone, I couldn't even speak for the tears and emotion. I didn't want to speak; I just wanted to stay within this overwhelming feeling of peace which was washing over me from the Lord. Mike handed me the mike and I couldn't say anything, I just gave it back to him. There was no need for me to tell everyone I was now a Christian; they could all see Him within me. I walked down into the water and was baptized in the name of Jesus Christ. Afterward I looked for Yvonne who looked even more like a small child who had been left out in the cold. Then her name was called out and without any hesitation she immediately made her way to the front of the church, took hold of the microphone and talked about what the Lord had done in her life for about ten minutes. She told stories which had the people in fits of laughter, there was no stopping her! I just stood there, still in the water, open mouthed. It was as though we had switched places, was this really my wife who moments before had been a dithering wreck? She finished talking and walked straight into the water beside me and was baptized. It didn't seem to bother her in the least when her head was ducked underwater. With tears of wonder and joy running down our faces we held each other. We both now knew that whatever fears and troubles and trials the enemy would throw our way, with God we would be strong enough to overcome them, the Lord was well and truly with us then and now.

Looking back at our baptism, it seemed God had, in fact, reversed mine and Yvonne's roles. He had given me the quietness and meekness of the Holy Spirit and to Yvonne He had given the confidence and boldness of the Holy Spirit because that's what we needed on that day. It's so true that the Lord provides!

Chapter 9

Miracles Never Cease

Today after many years if illness Yvonne is back to normal, she is the backbone of the family once more. The panic attacks have been replaced by a gentle confidence and she eats and enjoys her food once again. Her weight is normal and I now thank God for the miracle He performed in Yvonne's life. He gave me back my wife. Also he healed her of her epilepsy. She no longer takes fits. The Lord healed her. I know you find that hard to believe, but hey, that's why they are called miracles.

Talking of miracles, God didn't stop performing them after the Bible was printed, not so long ago I found a lump on one of my testicles, (if that word upsets anyone, I'm sorry). Anyway, I told Yvonne about it and after seeing for herself immediately rang the doctor. I began to make excuses at this point. I know a lot of people may have seen me on TV, may think I'm a bit brash and loud, but when it comes to personal matters such as this I am really very shy. In fact Yvonne laughs at me because as I turn off the light before undressing she has only rarely seen me naked during the whole of our marriage. She talked me into it and arranged for us to go and see the doctor the next day. We both knew that if anything was wrong it would be quite awkward as I was contracted to

appear in Great Yarmouth the very next day for the start
of a summer season. But we knew this was important so
rather than having it hanging over us we decided to get
it over with. We arrived at the surgery and the doctor
asked me in. This was going to be the first time that a
man would examine my private parts and so I have
never felt so embarrassed in my entire life. I tried to
make jokes to cover my shyness.

The doctor didn't even give me a glimmer of a smile
and it was getting more embarrassing by the moment.
After what seemed like far too long, he told me to get
dressed and informed me that he had found a lump that
shouldn't be there. He was worried and this worried me.
He said I was to see a specialist as soon as possible. I
explained my predicament. I had to be in Great
Yarmouth the very next day. He then made an appointment for me to see a doctor in Great Yarmouth and told
me I must see him as soon as I got there. I came straight
out with the million dollar question and asked him if it
was malignant or not. He obviously couldn't tell me
until further tests had been done. We went home that
day feeling very worried but for some reason we kept
our fears quiet from one another.

The next day after arriving in Great Yarmouth we
went straight to the doctors' surgery. Once again I had to
be embarrassingly examined. When he had finished he
told us that he had found the growth and that I was to
see a specialist who dealt with this kind of thing. Now he
had confirmed my worst fears, I did, in fact have a
growth and they were very concerned about it. I tried to
laugh it off with Yvonne but I could see she was worried.
We prayed together a lot during this period. The doctor
made us an appointment with the specialist for a week
later and I have to tell you that it was one of the longest
weeks of my life. Yvonne and I prayed before we set off
and trusted in the Lord. Once again at the specialists'
surgery, I was soon undressed and on the couch for the

examination. He probed and prodded for quite some time and then mentioned that there was another lump in addition to the first one which I had come across. He explained that he wasn't particularly worried about the first lump, but was very concerned about this second lump which he had found. He told me that he wanted me to go and have a scan to see what kind of growth we were dealing with.

We were devastated. Now there wasn't one growth, but two and even the specialist was concerned. We imagined the worst scenario, but even though it was completely out of character for both me and Yvonne, we kept all our fears to ourselves. The specialist arranged for us to go down to the hospital the very next day so we didn't have long to wait, but by the time we arrived we were both a bag of nerves. In the waiting area of the scan room we just sat there holding hands, we didn't speak but smiled weakly at each other. Eventually my name was called and after putting on my gown, the type which covers you, but only at the front, I was sent into another room where all the machinery was. In there was a man and a woman. Oh no, not a woman! Now a woman was going to see my prized possessions in every detail. This was my worst nightmare come true. The doctor asked me to sit down and then proceeded to put a type of jelly all over me. How much worse could this get! The nurse, thankfully, was over at the other side of the room, so at least I had that in my favour. He then began to take his photographs. I could see the doctor begin to frown. This didn't look good at all, I could see that he was worried and stared at the screen intensely. Eventually he gave up on this and came over and gave me a thorough physical examination. I watched his face as he, and I wouldn't wish this on any man, pulled, prodded and probed, I felt as though he was trying to pull the growths out manually. At long last he ceased his wrestling with me and went back to take some more pictures. After a while he called his nurse over to take a look. How embarrassing. There I lay like a turkey ready for Christmas and these two people were discussing the most personal part of my anatomy. They muttered and pointed and I heard him say, 'look at this, nurse', and 'perfect specimen' and even 'textbook material'. They were using medical terms, but they were talking about me. After much probing, puzzling and discussion, he came over and told me to sit up, which I did. He then told me he couldn't find anything wrong with me.

'In fact', he said, 'it is most puzzling, because I can't find any signs of a growth, even the scan didn't show up anything.'

I told him that three doctors had felt the growth, and one had felt two growths. He said that he knew this and that was what made it such a mystery to him, as the specialist who had sent me was highly respected and was never wrong about his diagnosis of these things. I felt utterly confused as I got dressed and left the room. Three doctors had felt the growth, even a specialist and now there was nothing there, not even a trace of one ever being there. Yvonne was waiting outside and looked up at me hopefully when I reached her. I told her that the scan was completely clear and what the doctor had said,

'My prayers have been answered!' she declared, extremely relieved.

The confusion that I had initially felt dissipated and I felt peace. I realized then that Yvonne had been praying and the Lord had answered. I found out later that Yvonne had telephone every Christian and every church we knew, and they had all been praying for me. There could be no other explanation, God had performed a miracle, and taken away the growths. Praise the Lord!

As I have said before, it wasn't until I became a Christian that I understood that there really is an enemy of our souls. One of the greatest deceptions the devil has put out is that he isn't real. But I now know that he is, and he doesn't like it when one of his disciples turn to Jesus and so goes on the attack. He will throw every temptation your way to discredit you and make you sinful, to turn you away from God. Anger, frustration, gossip, greed, selfish ambition are temptations that once entertained, become footholds for him, and once he gets a foothold, it soon turns into a stronghold.

Christians are not immune to these attacks and temptations, quite the contrary, there are times when he attacks us more, to try and discredit us. The difference is God always provides us with a way out of temptation. When I first became a Christian, I was full of the Lord and wanted to tell the world about it, so I started to do some gospel shows, just to tell as many people as I could the wonderful things God has done in my life. Every time I was going to set out to do them, Yvonne and I would have an argument over some minor trivial thing. We soon recognized that a spanner was being thrown in the works by the devil because I was going to talk about the Lord. Once I had fully understood this we could guard ourselves against such an attack, but we always have to be aware, as the enemy is an opportunist. But the greatest day of my life was when I found the Lord and kicked the devil in the face!

During my time with the Lord He has blessed me and done many great miracles in my life. Two years before this book was first written, something wonderful happened in my life, my daughter Joanne became a Christian. In the first version of this book I wrote that she had given her life on my birthday, while we were in a pub. But that was just the beginning, He showed her there, that He was real and a week or so later she prayed and committed her life to Him fully, while on her own in her front room. Now I know that some Christians say that I shouldn't be in a pub, but I believe that that's just where Jesus would be, should He be walking on this earth right now! He hung around with tax collectors and sinners and the authorities called Him a drinker! I have even felt condemned by being in show-business, with its pockets of homosexuality, alcoholism, drug addictions and adultery, not to mention all the seediness that is prevalent right now. Should I be among this, will I be tempted? Of course I will by some things! But if I keep my eyes on God, faith is my shield. God is faithful to give me a way out of temptation. Of course I also have to be wise and have to make the right choices, but I know that right now my place is in show-business, until I retire or God gives me something else to do. I am not saying that we should all march into pubs and knock people over their heads with a Bible, but being real and strong, but gentle as Jesus Himself showed. Believe me, if you are truly walking with the Lord, He will shine through, and when people know you are a Christian, they inevitably ask questions. There is a hunger out there which needs to be satisfied, who knows, just by telling someone you are a Christian can begin a chain of events which could lead to the next Billy Graham being saved!

Well, on that night in the pub, I was out with my wife and children and their partners and as usual the conversation turned to the Lord. They always became interested and would fire questions at me. Joanne suddenly got up and walked away, saying she was going to the ladies, she had been quiet all night so Yvonne followed her. I carried on talking to the boys. Eventually they came back and I could see that Joanne was emotional. Yvonne told me that she had prayed for Joanne in the ladies room and I thought, just by looking at her that she had just given her life to the Lord, I was ecstatic. But as I said before, it was only the beginning, Yvonne had prayed for her, but Joanne hadn't prayed, or accepted Jesus to be her savior yet. That happened about a week later, she prayed out loud on her own to God and He met her right there and saved her. God doesn't worry about where we are, if we admit we are sinners and are sorry and, acknowledging who He is, turn our lives over to Him, He is faithful and just to forgive us and we become brand new creations. Isn't He a wonderful God!

My Joanne is now a committed Christian with very strong beliefs, God has done some marvelous things in her life and she is hungry for whatever God wants to do. What is marvelous is that she teaches me things. We can have some very long discussions! God has truly blessed her with wisdom beyond her years.

God moved mightily in Joanne's life one day. She was expecting her third child Joel when she was told there was a problem. They told her at the hospital that they wanted to give her an amniocentesis because from the scan they had four markers to suggest that the baby was going to have a chromosome disorder which they believed would most likely to turn out to be Down-syndrome. Joanne did not agree to the test because of further risk to the baby and for her it wouldn't have made any difference as she would never have terminated the pregnancy. The doctors suggested that she should be scanned every two weeks and were shocked to see her when she arrived a fortnight later as they had expected the pregnancy to miscarry. At this stage they believed the baby to be severely handicapped but hadn't quite ruled out the possibility of Down syndrome. The hospital sent her to a specialist in Manchester for a more thorough scan and the doctor there strongly urged that Joanne abort the baby, at this stage she was quite far on in her pregnancy, and ignoring her refusals, the doctor went on to state that as they considered the baby to be mentally handicapped as well as physically, she would legally be able to terminate. Joanne would not consider it and intensified her prayers. She gave it all to God. Yvonne and I also started to pray that if it was God's will then we needed His peace on the situation, but Joanne would not believe it was Gods will. It all seemed strange those nine months of Joanne's expectancy because the more we prayed, more problems surfaced with the baby, but all these things needed prayer and the church all around the country seemed to join with us. Joanne had twelve scans in all and I personally saw the last scan and saw with my own eyes that the baby was in a real mess.

Joel was born one week after I saw that scan and he was absolutely PERFECT. God has completely healed him. Nobody knew what to expect, but during the whole time God showed Joanne that she had to trust Him. I see a walking miracle everyday. He is five years old now and a normal happy boy. Praise God.

I believe that one day I will be heaven with Yvonne, Joanne and Robert and Darren, all my grandkids; my whole family. Isn't God great?

I've said a lot about my family, but you may be wondering about Tommy. I first told his wife Hazel that I had become a Christian on a plane and she had thought that it was another one of my hair-brained schemes. She thought, 'give it a couple of weeks or so to get it out of his system and he'll be fine!' She admitted that she didn't think much about it and didn't understand it, but she did see a drastic change in me over a space of time, not as aggressive and, she said, she saw that I had an inner peace which amazed her, but even after I told her how it all happened, she didn't really want to know or understand at that point. After about four years, though, she told me that she used to think I was 'much better this way' and she hoped I wouldn't revert back to how I was before.

With Tommy, he said he thought I was a crackpot. He just couldn't believe it and thought it was all just a big cop-out when I told him that I'd been forgiven for my sins. He just couldn't believe that after the way I had been, that I could be forgiven. That was how he thought from the very beginning. I asked him if it had annoyed him at all and he said it didn't really bother him either way. When he went out and played golf with his friends they would ask him, 'What's going on with Bobby and this Christian stuff?' and he would say to them, 'Hey, it's his own thing.' And that's about as far as it affected him. Hazel and Tommy discussed it together, but came to the conclusion it was just a phase and that I'd get over it one day. Tommy explained to me, however, that he never really dismissed Christianity for himself, but was more indifferent to the whole idea. He didn't see an immediate change, but over the next four or five years the change was very big. At the very beginning, although the way I treated others had changed, I still needed to work on my temperament. Old habits do die hard and Tommy at first thought to himself that no way was I a Christian, I still sometimes swore within the act, and then he told me that suddenly he noticed a peacefulness about me which he liked, and he then decided that whatever it was I had, was great! He saw that I was a changed person and began to want some of it. He even admitted that maybe he was a bit jealous of what I had, but in the early days, I was still learning, now he sees that I'm a different person, he says, 'It's like chalk and cheese between what you used to be and what you are now.'

Tom once said to me that he was a Christian and I turned around and told him that he wasn't. This, he said, made him feel really confused as in his own eyes; he had always been a Christian. He went to church as a child, was brought up to believe in God and lived in a Christian country. He admitted that he always thought that there was 'something' out there, but supposed he could sort it all out when he was dead, or about to die. He asked me about God and I wondered whether it was to try and trip me up. The question he asked was, 'If a murderer met God, would God forgive him?' He had read this question in a magazine in a doctors' surgery and immediately decided to come and ask me. I told him that if the murderer turned from his sin and asked for the Lord's forgiveness then he would be forgiven. At that time

Tommy didn't understand this, but told me that it was through this question, that he wanted to know more.

On November 8th 1992, Tommy and I were working at a place in South Wales. It wasn't far from Kings Church, Newport, which my friend Ray Bevin is Pastor of. My daughter Joanne decided to come along and have her son Christian dedicated to the Lord. Ray arranged everything and it was all planned to be held on the morning during the service. About a week before we were due to go, Yvonne suggested that we ask Tom and Hazel if they would like to go with us and if they wanted, they could dedicate their daughter, Kelly. I suggested this and Tommy flatly refused. I decided to leave it, and didn't bother asking again. But, surprise, surprise, a couple of days later Tommy asked if it would be possible to arrange it. I was overjoyed; this was an answer from God. I told him no problem and we sorted out the details. It was the first time Tommy had been to a church like The King's Church. It is a wonderful place and filled with the Holy Spirit. Ray is a good Pastor and makes the word of God understandable for the non-believer. The music is great and I knew that Tommy could not fail to be impressed.

When we arrived, we spent a few minutes with Ray in his office. He gave us a cup of tea and explained what would happen at the dedication. Ray tried to put Tommy and Hazel at ease, but I could tell that they were far from comfortable. I could understand it really. They were surrounded by born-again Christians, not fully understanding what it all meant, it seemed so different to the old style church, they must have been worried that they had walked into some kind of cult. They obviously felt like outsiders, which is a lie from hell. As His creation, we belong where God is.

When we went into the church to found our seats and a man came boldly, and gave Tommy a big bear hug and said, 'Bless you Tommy.'

This threw Tommy totally, if he wasn't sure if we were all crackpots before, he certainly did now. He was so embarrassed. I saw the look on his face and he just didn't know what to do. I chuckled to myself; I knew that God was hitting him on the head!

As we sang, I took a sneaky look at Tommy and Hazel, and they were singing at the top of their voices. At the end of the worship time Ray asked us to go up to the front as he would dedicate the children. It was wonderful, a very special day and well worth waiting for. After the dedication, we all sat down and Ray began to preach. He spoke on the forgiveness of sins and coming to the Lord. Tommy was listening intently, so I began to pray. Yvonne and I, along with a few others had been praying for a while for Tommy and Hazel and the Lord had answered some of my prayers by just getting them in there. It was a very powerful message, and I could see that it had an effect on Tommy. At the end Ray asked us all to bow our heads and asked if there was anyone in that room who wanted to commit their lives to the Lord and be forgiven for their sins to simply raise their hands. Every head in the church was bowed and I didn't dare look at Tommy and Hazel, I was too busy praying for them and another member of my family who was there. It would be beyond my wildest dreams for them to join us on our journey with the Lord. Suddenly Yvonne dug me in the ribs; I stopped praying and looked at her wondering what was up. She looked at me with tears in her eyes and nodded in Tommy and Hazel's direction. Their hands were up in the air.

I could hardly believe it! I cannot begin to describe what I felt. It was a tremendous sense of joy. Tears began to run down my face, I was so pleased for them, not to mention that now I would no longer be a crackpot to Tommy! Thank-you Lord. All these years we'd been close one minute, falling out the next, distant from each other, sometimes jealous, then close again, it was like a cycle, but now we are brothers. God has answered my prayers. Ray then asked those who had put up their hands to go forward so that he could pray for them. By this time Yvonne and I were in tears. It was glorious, what a wonderful thing to see.

Afterward I could actually see the weight that had gone from Tommy's shoulders. When we left church that day, both Tommy and Hazel were different, they had peace. Since then we have been mocked and jeered at because we are Christians, but, you know, I did it myself before I knew the Lord. I hope that those who do check it out for themselves before they go along with the crowd, they might see just what they're missing. Fame and fortune are not life, nor are they the answer to all the problems in the world, God is.

My life has been a series of ups and downs. But since 1986, my life has been on the up. So many wonderful things have happened to me since I found God. I am not talking about material things or career success; but spiritually. I have found a great sense of peace. All I want to do now is get closer to the Lord. I know that some people will not understand this, but that's fine, I know what I mean. Tommy and I have never been part of the show business clique (and, oh yes, there is one), at one time, it used to bother me and I thought it was because we were northern, or because we didn't act like we had power, as some stars do, I don't know, maybe it was God keeping us safe from the trappings of all that, but it no longer bothers me, I belong to a bigger 'club'. Everything seems trivial when I look at the magnitude of God. It hurts me when I hear everyone blaming Him for all the pain and suffering in the world, when we cause most of it.

I'm very contented, much more than I ever have been. I look at Yvonne and she gets prettier every day. I know it might sound soppy, but it's the truth, and when I look back on what my life once was. I thank God that He kept us together. Every day it is wonderful to wake up and know that I have my family around me, and if there is a crisis, everyone pulls together. Through show business I could have lost every one of them, so I thank God that He has blessed me with these people. He has shown me that one kiss from my wife is worth more than anything, because she is kissing me with real love.

Many men think that drinking, womanizing, fighting and clawing their way up power-mountains is the way that life should be lived. Well I believe they are wrong, I know because I have been there. If these people are truly honest with themselves and look deep into their hearts they would find that they are not truly happy, something is missing. That something is God. No-one can be truly happy until they've found Him. He fills that little space within, which nothing or no-one else can ever fill. We try to fill it with all sorts of rubbish and that is dangerous and leads to addictions to whatever it is that gives them a short term fulfillment, we simply self destruct. Then there are those who think that because they are basically a nice person, God will have a little stock take at the end of their lives and if the good outweighs the bad, He'll forgive them for the sins they committed when they were alive. What a chance to take with your eternal existence! I know that I'd rather be assured of an eternity in heaven than an eternity in hell.

A person who has found God does not fear death, nor do they have a vague hope. They have fact! Jesus taught that when we are forgiven, we will live with Him and I believe the Bible is true.

Other people may say that becoming a Christian is taking the easy way out and God wants us to stand on our own two feet. I don't think He does. He says give everything to Him and He will help us with all things, if you think that's easy, try it. Giving every part of your life over to God is a challenge and we have to do it daily.

There are also those who say that to be a Christian all you have to do is good works and go to church and pray.

It takes a lot more than that. The first step is to make a commitment to the Lord, asking Him to forgive your sins and inviting Him into your life. Allow me to illustrate what I mean;

If you have a bottle and fill it with milk, but leave some of the old milk in the bottom, then the old milk will curdle the new. That is why we must thoroughly wash the bottle first, (us) with the Holy Spirit, before we can pour the new (life) into it. In other words we must ask the Lord to take away our old life before we can begin a new one. We don't have to work and do as many good deeds as we can to gain the favour of God. If we are new and God is within us, they will come naturally. The Lord gives His gift of a new life freely, it is ours to take. It was given by Jesus dying on the cross, taking the blame for our sins. He then defeated death by rising up again and there the enemy was defeated.

I know people think that all this is easy for me to say, thinking that I have a lot of money. Well I have to destroy this myth; I have no piles of money! I have to work to pay my mortgage and bills with the rest of the population. But I am far happier now than when I was rich. In fact my riches are not in money at all. I would sooner have just one drop of the Lord's grace in my life than a whole bank full of money.

The old life that I used to lead of womanizing, drinking and fighting seems alien to me now. I can never understand now how I or anyone else could be like that. But God has removed me so far away from that life by His grace and the good news is that He can do this for anyone. No matter what we might have done, God loves us all.

Since humbling myself and committing my spirit and soul to the Lord he has taken me on a fantastic journey. As I said earlier there have been mountains to climb, but with God holding our hands we have climbed them. He took what talent he has given me and used it to glorify

Him, which is how it should be. For the past ten years I take about 4 months a year to travel around churches to give my testimony and it is great to see how God ministers to the needs of the people.

He has given me three wonderful children, nine marvelous grandkids (up to now) and a fantastic wife. I thank him everyday for what he has done for me. Don't get me wrong it hasn't been all a bed of roses, there have been many trials and tribulations, but hey if we didn't have to go through troubles then how would we grow.

Chapter 10

I'm a Celebrity get
me out of here

One of the most interesting moments in my life was when I was asked would I be interested in joining 11 other people for a reality show set in the jungle in Australia. The show is called 'I'm a Celebrity get me out of here,' and it is a huge success in England. It comprises of 12 celebrities being thrown together in a jungle on the other side of the world and made to survive. All they are allowed to eat each day was 4 spoonfuls of rice each per day and some Soya beans. That is it! Oh and lest I forget you can drink as much water as you wanted. The water where we were came from a stream which ran beside the camp and had to be boiled, and then put in a canvas bag. So you can tell by this description the water was by no means a treat. To get meals for the rest of the camp, food the celebrities have to perform 'Bush tucker trials.' These clever trials consisted of many different tests as diverse as eating beetles, mealworms and kangaroo testicles to being made to pedal specially made cycles 50ft above the canopy of the jungle. When the tests had been completed then the contestants in this 'reality show' would be awarded extra food to the amount of how much of the trial had been completed. Why it was called a reality show I'll never know because there is nothing real about living in a jungle and eating kangaroo testicles. When I was offered a chance appear in 'I'm a celebrity get out of here' I was overjoyed, because,

A. I was offered a substantial amount of money.

B. It gave me the chance of an adventure.

Also my partner Tom and been asked to appear so it wasn't going to be too bad, I wouldn't be on my own, or so I thought.

Tom and I arrived in the jungle via helicopter mid afternoon. I had never before been in a rainforest, now I know why they are called that. I have never seen as much rain. It was like the sky had opened and decided to release all the rain it had stored up since time began. We greeted by an actor called Sid Owen and a singer called Jenny Frost from a girl band called Atomic Kitten. They made us really welcome and guided us to the camp. The journey was a nightmare because of the rain. It had made the forest floor like a mud bath so we were sliding down on our bums or trying to climb, with the help of trees, our way up. We eventually after about a mile of climbing hit the camp. We were greeted by the rest of the competitors. These were; antique dealer David Dickinson, Carol Thatcher, a writer and the daughter Margaret Thatcher, Anthony Costa from a boy band called Blue, wine expert Jilly Goolden, British actress Sheree Murphy, Australian actress Kimberly Davis and living legend Jimmy Osmond. What can I say about Jimmy? He one of the nicest people I have ever met.

They are all such a great bunch of people and it was my privilege to meet them. They all made us really welcome, and the strange is that this program, along with most reality shows, are created in a way that encourages the people to argue, but we never did really. There were only a couple of times when tempers got frayed – but no big fall-outs. It must have driven the producers mad, and they tried lots of tricks to make us angry. But, interestingly, what happened was that this series we were in pulled in two million more viewers than the previous series. I thought it was a great message to the big bosses of television land that people still enjoy good, wholesome family entertainment. Anyway we settled in very quickly and Tom and I did our first bush tucker trial.

Tom and I had been chosen for a bush tucker trial straight away in our stay in the jungle so we set out on our trek to where we had to do it, again climbing, slipping and sliding up and down through the bush. When we arrived at our predestined spot my heart dropped because we had to pedal this cycle-like contraption which was attached to a high-wire and collect as many stars as we could along the way, each star representing a meal for our co-campers. Now that doesn't sound too bad but we were about 100ft above the forest floor, and this contraption didn't feel too safe. It swung about, up and down and there was nothing beneath us but an enormous space between us and the jungle. Deep inside I knew it was safe but my mind was telling me it wasn't. I have never been as frightened in my life. All I could shout for some reason and I don't know why was Von, Von, Von, Von (my name for Yvonne). Anyway to cut a long story short Tom and I peddled for our lives and we managed to collect 9 stars which meant 9 meals for the people back in the camp. When we got back to the camp we were treated like heroes. We had started to bond with the other people there but it wasn't long before disaster struck, well for me anyway.

We hadn't been in the camp long when Tom was voted out. I couldn't believe it. I was sat there when they announced his name. My whole world seemed to collapse. There he was, my best mate, being voted out of the camp. He put a brave face on but I could tell that he was absolutely crushed. He was devastated and so was

I, but Tommy is Tommy and he smiled through his pain. When he had gone I felt a deep sense of loneliness. Even though there were people around me I felt as if I had been left out on my own. Tom and I had started this together and I wanted to finish it together. I also knew now that I had to pick my emotions off the floor and start getting stuck in. after I had decided to pick myself of the floor things got better. Even though it was hot and wet I started to enjoy my time in the jungle. We would go to bed when it went dark and get up when it got light. I now realize we were going to bed around 7 at night and getting up at around 4 in the morning. I was always the first up and I would try to get fire lit again. It gave a tremendous feeling of achievement when the first flickers of flame came alive. Simple things eh? I will always remember on night we had a thunder storm and I had never seen one like it, in fact I had never been in rain forest during a thunderstorm. The lightening was all around us and we were caught in a torrential downpour. We all gathered together under a canopy and waited for the storm to pass. We could hear trees around us falling where the lightening had hit them and we were sure the producers would pull us out, but they didn't. The storm eventually bated and we went to our individual beds. They were wet through and we had to sleep in them. This was impossible, so we re-lit the fire and put our sleeping bags out to dry. I think we only slept for about one hour that night. The next morning it was as though there had never been storm. The sun was shining through the trees and it felt glorious to be alive. The only sign of a storm was the river that ran by the side of the camp, it was like raging rapids. Nobody had seen Carol but we weren't un-duly bothered because she had a habit of wandering off, so I went get some logs from the firewood pile that was situated down in the forest. I set off and when I reached the river, lo and behold there was Carol sat in the middle of the river on camping chair reading something. She was sunbathing. It was the most surreal thing I had seen.

"Morning Bobby," she said, as if it was the most normal thing in the world, but then again I suppose it was to Carol. She is a 'one-off', and I feel privileged to have met her.

The jungle was a crazy wonderful place to be and you do have a tendency to forget that the camera's are on you 24/7. Sometimes things happen that to us in the jungle was nothing like the viewers at home saw it, and it is only when you get out of the jungle and you are told things that you realize. I was closest to Anthony Costa, Carol and Sheree Murphy. Sheree and I would banter together and make each other laugh. I'd pretend to flirt with her and go over the top by saying things like she had lovely eyes and that I liked her left one best. Stuff like that, and she started to mother me. Now I suffer from a bad neck and most of the people in the camp rubbed it at some point or another but Sheree and Jenny would mostly rub it, but it was Sheree that I would laugh most with. One day along, with Sid, we put a face pack on each other made from avocados and honey. I don't like avocados to begin with so this was disgusting to me. Now before you start saying 'that's a bit soft isn't it?' it was something we were told to do. Anyway she put the face pack on and just giggled and laughed and sneakily tried to eat it, we were that hungry. Well, unknown to me, as we had no outside contact, the producers had gone to Yvonne and told there that they were worried because 'there was a bit of flirting in the jungle'. They had taken it seriously! Yvonne just laughed and said 'it's Bob isn't it?' when they said yes she told them not to worry, and said, 'he has always been like that,' she knew there was nothing in it. What a belter! Yvonne and I have kept in touch with Sheree and her husband as well as Anthony and Carol and some of the other campmates, they even came all the way up to Hull to see me and

Tommy in Pantomime and it was a great pleasure to see them without any cameras and microphones listening to our conversations!

During my time in the jungle, I started to pine for Yvonne big time. I was desperate to see her and because it wasn't the 'be all and end all' for me to win it made it worse. Every morning when Ant and Dec, the presenters, arrived to say who had been voted out when it wasn't me my heart would sink to rock bottom for about an hour then I would pick myself up again. How could I miss this woman that much after 32 years of marriage? That in itself must be a miracle. Anyway the days came and went and people were being voted out except me and I was reaching desperation point. Then one morning after 11 days and nights in the jungle Ant and Dec came. They looked at each of us and said,

"Bobby it's you! You have been voted out!"

They were like words from Heaven. I had been bitten by spiders, I was bitten from head to toe by mosquitoes, I was constipated and had diarrhea at the same time, I didn't know whether I was coming or going. I was ravenous for food and now I was eventually going to see my Yvonne. I packed my things very quickly and said my farewells to the companions I had just spent 11 days with and I was out of there. When I reached the long rope ladder that leads us out of the jungle I saw Yvonne. It was something from an old movie. It felt like there was music playing and we were in slow motion. We ran across the rope bridge towards each other and when we met she said,

"You don't know what I have been through."

I felt like throwing her off the bridge! I had been through the strangest time of my life, completely cut off from the outside world and I didn't know what she'd been through? She told me after because I didn't know that all the families had to be up at four in the morning and travel about an hour and half to the jungle to see if their loved one is coming out. Well Yvonne did this for 11 days and also because I had shouted Von, Von, Von, it had become a little catchphrase in England so she was on the television and in the press all the time. Now Yvonne is very much a background person and suddenly she had been thrown into the spotlight and had had interviews with magazines, newspapers and T.V. She hated it, but we survived. Yes the jungle was something I will never forget. I loved it. I met some great people and it changed my life in more ways than one.

It also brought me closer to God. It made me realize that if we could let God take control of out lives and we submit to him. Then His plan for our lives would phenomenal.

Chapter 11

The Plan

Whether we believe it or not God has a plan for our lives. It is glorious plan if only we would humble ourselves to God and let him be the leader of our lives and then his plan for us would come to fruition, but I know as well as you do that is hard to do, because we like to be in control. That is why God's plan for our lives sometimes never seems to become a reality because we are too busy planning our lives for ourselves. It's true isn't it? We plan everything except for what is going to happen to us after death. We plan what we are having for tea, what we are going to watch on television, where we are going for our holidays. Now there's a thing, planning our holidays. Usually it's the wife that goes to the travel agents and comes back with mound of travel brochures that you could paper a house with, but we always end up going to Tenerife or the same old place. Remember we have planned this. The wives usually pack the suitcases and have you noticed guys that when the wives pack the cases our clothes are always at the bottom and they always say 'we'll get an iron when we get there.' Anyway the big day comes and we reach the airport, and if you are frightened of flying the first sign we see is Terminal! Well that's a good start. Anyway we get into the airport and then onto the airplane. Now I have a problem on airplanes because Yvonne always puts the hand luggage up in the overhead lockers and people look at me as if I am lazy. What they don't know is that I can't reach being vertically challenged. Then we finally get settled and the air hostess begins her instructions about the exit doors. It's when she comes to the part about having flotation devices under our seats that bothers me, because if we are crashing I don't want a life jacket, I want a parachute. Why can't they put parachutes instead of life jackets under the seats? I would be a happier traveler. Anyway we eventually reach Tenerife and then we wait ages for our cases to arrive of the plane then we drag them out into the blistering sun. Our next mammoth task is to find a taxi to take us to our accommodation. Remember, we have planned this. We eventually get a cab and then our Spanish accents kicks in, and funny enough everything seems to end in the letter O. 'Excusio Taxio, can you take us the hotelio? And how mucheo? They must think we're crackers. After much misunderstanding we are on our way. We settle in and after a couple of days we are looking like boiled lobsters. We have over sun-bathed and we can hardly walk for pain. Then diarrhoea sets in and we are running around like burned head-less chickens. The holiday ends and we arrive home to the inevitable question 'did you have a good time?' to which we reply 'it was marvelous.' Remember we planned that. God's plan for us is bigger than anything we can imagine. And also remember that whatever we do in life, we pick it up and carry it. It is only when we accept Jesus Christ as our savior that we are truly free from the sins that we carry

I want to leave you with this scenario. Imagine that we are on the highway of life with an empty suitcase and on either side of the highway are travel agents, tempting us with their wares. We see the first travel agents 'Lust Locations'. I spent many years in there, filling up my suitcase with all sorts of vices. When we leave we find that our suitcase is a little heavier. Then we see another travel agent 'Pride Paradise' we go into this place and fill our suitcase with lots of pride. We leave there and we another travel agent 'Greed Getaway's' we enter this place and greedily fill our suitcase to over-flowing. We look down the highway and see many different travel agents, 'Anger Airways', 'Envy Holidays', 'Gossip Go', 'Steal Sun-ways', and many more. We spend most of our lives going in and out of these travel agencies and all the time our suitcase is getting heavier and heavier. We keep passing a little travel agent with not much in the window but a rainbow, which doesn't look as inviting as the other travel agents so we are not bothered about going in, but some of us are curious, so we go in. when we get in the shop we are greeted by a very nice man who says,

"Oh hello, I so happy you have come in. I have been waiting for you."

"Well, it's good to be here," we answer, out of politeness, "So tell me," we continue

"What's heaven like?"

"Oh, "the man replies "it's fantastic. It's that good, no-one has ever come back."

"Really!" we say "Have you been?"

"Yes." Replies the man

"Well why did you come back?" we ask

"I had to do," he replies "It's My Fathers business."

"What is the accommodation like in Heaven?" we ask.

"Oh it's mansions." He replies.

"And how much is it too go." We ask.

"Oh it's free," he replies "I bought your ticket many years ago."

"Really," we say, now very interested "How much did it cost?"

"My life." He replies.

"Oh!" we answer in a mild state of shock.

We think about what he has just said for a few moments, realizing that no-one has ever done anything of that magnitude for us before, and if he did that he must have truly loved us. We look at the man and see this enormous amount of love surrounding him, and we are drawn towards him.

"Well, I've made up my mind," we eventually say "I have been in all those other travel agencies and my suitcase is full of all their wares, and now I realize that this one is by far the best."

"I know," he says "I have been watching you."

"Really," we reply "Well I would like to go Heaven if that's okay with you."

"Well let me look in your suitcase first." He says.

We look down at our suitcase and realize just how heavy it has been and we are surprised at all the weight we have been carrying around.

"Well," we stutter in embarrassment "it's so heavy I can't get it up onto the desk."

He smiles "leave it with me, "he says, and picks up the heavy suitcase with one hand and lifts it onto the desk.

He opens the suitcase. "Oh, "he says, taking out a pair of underpants "some underpants of lust, and a shirt of greed, oh and look here," he continues "a vest of anger, and some socks of gossip."

He continues to empty the suitcase of all the things that we have picked up on our walk on the highway of life. Eventually our suitcase is empty.

"Well," we say, a little disappointed "we can't go to heaven now, we have nothing to take."

"Now," he says "you are absolutely perfect to go; you see I will provide all you will ever need to get to heaven."

He turns and hands us something that looks like a book.

"This," he continues "is the brochure for Heaven, take it outside, read it and then come back and tell me if you still want to go to heaven."

We take the brochure and go out onto the highway of life. We suddenly notice a lot of people going in and out of the travel agents carrying very heavy suitcases, and everyone of them is looking like they are dissatisfied, and they seem to have a urgency about them as if they are looking for something. We realize that we must appear that way. Then we see some other people walking around with the brochure for Heaven tucked under their arms and they look totally different. They have a sort of peace about them, a sense of knowing something we don't.

We look down at the brochure that the man has given us and we see that it is called The Bible. We wonder what the word Bible means? Could it mean?

B – Basic
I – Instructions
B – Before
L – Leaving
E – Earth?

Well whatever it means we feel we want to read it. When we start to read it we realize that all those things it talks about anger, lust, hate, greed, gossip, malice, pride and many more things are us. We have been carrying those things because we have picked them up at the other travel agents and they had become our way of life. Then we realize that the guy we had been speaking too in the travel agents was indeed Jesus Christ. We read how he died this horrendous death so that we could be free from all those things were going to take us to death, and that through him we could ever-lasting life. We realize that only through him could we ever, ever get to Heaven.

We pick up our Bible and rush back to the Jesus shop. We burst in.

"Please," we cry "I want to go to Heaven. I wish I had found your many years ago then I would not have gone in those other places. I know who you are now. You are Jesus. Please Jesus forgive me."

Jesus smiles and takes hold of our hands and we see the nail holes in his, "Do you regret going in all those other places?" he asks

"Oh yes, Jesus," we cry "I want to spend my life with you. I accept you Jesus as my Lord and Saviour."

We see a tear roll down Jesus cheek. He has been waiting so long for us.

"Have you got your passport?" he asked

We hand him our 'life' passport and it is ripped and battered from all the tribulations we have been through in life. He takes our battered passport and throws it away. He opens our hands and into them places a brand new passport.

"It has been stamped," he says "Now you are ready to go to heaven."

We open the passport and we see that it is truly indeed stamped and the stamp says 'Forgiven.' We take our treasured passport and head for the airport, when we arrive at the airport we see all the travel agents gates empty. There is no-one there, because everybody is trying to get through the 'Heaven Holiday's' gate. Some people are trying to bribed their way through, some are begging, some are crying, some are threatening, but it's all too no avail. We take our passport to the gate and someone says,

"Oh you have met Jesus, go through."

We go through and we see the duty free, and it is really free. We start to fill our empty suitcase up with the gifts of Jesus.

Folks I am in the departure lounge of life and I have a brand new passport. Have you?

If not, then go to Jesus today in fact put this book down and come with me now and get your passport. It is the only way we get to heaven.

If you feel after reading this book you want Jesus in

your life then say this simple prayer. But say it with all
your heart,

'Dear Father
I come to you as a sinner and I ask you to forgive my
  sins
I truly repent of what I have done and ask you to fill
  my life right now with your love
I ask you Father to give me new life today and wash
  me in Jesus blood
And I think you Lord for sending your son to die for
  me
So I ask you once again Father to forgive me
And I accept Jesus Christ as my Lord and Savior
Amen